Grandma
Tell Us
a Story

IMPORTANT NOTICES

Grandma Tell Us a Story

Tales of a Daring Hypochondriac

Marion Pollack

Dedication

I was born on December 16, 1938.

So now you know my age.

We can argue forever the definition and real meaning of age, especially old age. No one wants to get old, but we can take comfort in knowing it is universally inescapable.

I dedicate this book to the people of my generation. We have had a great run during the best of times. You have your own memorable experiences and lots of old photographs to prove it. You have stories too, which should be preserved.

So this is my challenge to you.

Write it down. Write a memoir anthology.

Do it with poetry, song, and stories.

Tell it in your own voice.

Take the risk.

Your family will love it.

Contents

Contents, cont'd

Contents, cont'd

Introduction

This writing adventure is a tribute to my family past and present.

Writing these stories and poems has helped me sort out my family history. It has also helped me better understand myself and the world. Now I want to share what I have learned.

When a tiny particle of memory shows up I write it down. Before I know it one thought leads to another. Suddenly there is a story.

My mother wrote charming little stories about the history of our family. She gave us enough glimpses of herself to feed our imaginations. Now that her stories are preserved for posterity, I have begun to wonder about the secrets she only touched on. I love to picture her life as a child, as a teenager, and as the adult she was before I was born.

My father wrote an autobiography. I have added dialogue and some detail in hopes of bringing it to life. It is interesting to note that when I first found it I read it only superficially because I wanted to protect myself from his painful story. When I began to transcribe his work I became completely enthralled. I was transported to his early life in Austria and his difficult journey to America.

I have finished as much as I'm going to write for now. I want to share my stories and poems with my family and friends. Over the last six years, I have sent pertinent pieces to people I thought would appreciate them. I love it when someone close to me remembers an event that touches them or sparks a memory.

I enjoy it more when they get to laugh or shed a tear.

Best yet is when my teenaged grandchildren read my stories and are moved by them.

Their responses are precious to me.

I hope you will be moved or laugh with them also.

Childhood

A person's a person no matter how small.
— *Dr. Suess*

With Mom and Dad

Mommy, I Don't Want to Go to School

In the beginning, it is the three of us, Mom, Dad and me.
Such a neat, funny little family. We do everything together, trips, museums, shows, and restaurants.

I love our outings to the Bronx Zoo. I especially love riding on Dad's shoulders when I feel tired.

Schooling starts at home. By age three my father, who has strict Austrian manners, teaches me to eat properly.

"Marion dear, you must never touch the food on your plate. You must always use proper utensils. It's barbaric to shovel food with your thumb."

He shows me how to point my index fingers on both the knife and the fork in order to cut my food. I am to sit up straight, place a napkin on my lap and carefully chew small bits with my mouth closed. I may never speak with food in my mouth or place my elbows on the table. Dad quickly knocks my arms to my lap if I do.

I am a good girl.

By age four, we have moved to apartment 4B at 11 Metropolitan Oval, Parkchester, the Bronx. We love our new modern apartment with parquet floors and a roaring flush toilet. Life is sweet. The three of us play board games, mom reads me wonderful books. I paint pictures and help Mom and Dad cook.

In the way of all good things, it has to end.

"Marion, you are four years old, it's time to go to nursery school."

"But why mommy? I don't want to go to school. I have friends upstairs and downstairs too, right here in our building."

"All children go to nursery school. You'll like all the fun things they do there."

So I agree. I am a good girl.

When the day of doom arrives, I am nauseated and nervous. In my bedroom, the sickeningly upbeat voice of John Gambling comes on the radio. I smell the oatmeal cooking.

Oh no, Mommy is coming to wake me.

I pretend to be asleep.

"Rise and shine, Marion. Time to get up to go to school." she sings.

"Mommy, I feel sick."

I barely gag down the oatmeal mom prepares. We take the bus a few stops to the school.

"I'll pick you up at noon. Have fun."

I shyly meet the teacher and the children. I look down at the planks of wood beneath my feet and wipe my sweaty hands on

4

my dress. The teacher leads me to a group of children sitting on the floor in a circle passing around a big ball. If you miss you are out. It is going well and the game speeds up. The boy sitting next to me slaps the ball out of my hand.

"You're out!" He screams and everyone laughs. I am mortified and get up with tears in my eyes. The teacher sees this and leads me to a low sink filled with sudsy water and lots of plastic plates and bowls, where another little girl is washing dishes.

"You can dry," she says.

"Ok."

This is fun for me and I even get a turn to wash. Soon I am giggling with this girl. We are friends. All too soon the teacher changes the activity.

"It's snack and nap time children" she sings. It's 11:00 a.m., an hour before mom picks me up. The snack is graham crackers and milk that tastes sour. We go into the nap room where I see rows of cots.

"This is your cot, Marion."

I lie down. There is no pillow and the cot has a moldy smell. I miss my own blanket and pillow. I lie stiffly on my back trying to think of pleasant things. There is no way I can sleep here.

At 11:30 everyone wakes up and we go outside to play. There are swings, slides, seesaws and a jungle gym. I always like going down the slide and I love to climb. The little girl I did dishes with asks me to ride the seesaw with her. We precariously balance to get on and enjoy the up and down motion. The boy who knocked the ball out of my hands comes up behind me and holds my side down.

"Stop it!" I yell. He is laughing hysterically.

"Let me go!" I scream.

Suddenly and with great force, he jerks me upward. More frightened than hurt, I topple to the ground. My little girlfriend lands with a loud bump. I will later notice black and blue marks on my thigh and arm. I am crying uncontrollably when the teacher comes by to wipe my tears and give me a lemon drop.

It is time to go home. Mom is waiting right on time. I run into her arms.

I refuse to ever go back to that school. Mom and Dad agree to let me stay home and I take art lessons instead.

Am I a bad girl?

I Love My Friends

By second grade I have gained the confidence to walk the fifteen blocks to PS 102 with my friends. I love my Parkchester friends.

At school, I hold my nose as I walk past the lunchroom, with its disgusting odors of tomato soup and peanut butter sandwiches. I skip down the hall knowing I will find comfort in Miss Van Buren's second-grade class.

Each day we practice making circles in the air to prepare for cursive writing. Then, for weeks, we draw slants and curly lines on paper until finally, we form real and perfect letters. Signing our names in cursive is a gift. I feel like an artist!

Every school year brings new adventures and reasons to accelerate my anxiety. I am learning to cope.

Fifth grade is memorable because, besides copying endless arithmetic problems and reading out loud from the basal reader, we have a very odd teacher. Her name is Mrs. New. She has white fluffy hair and is extremely fat. Her enormous breasts extend beyond any normal human phenomena.

She always has her bare feet in a basin of warm water under her desk.

If you are one of her favorites you get to carry the basin down the hall for a refill. I am never chosen.

One day, to my surprise Mrs. New says,

"Marion, you have been very good, so you may refill my water basin. Make sure the water is warm."

With great delight, I skip down the hall to the girl's room, carrying the basin. I fill it with warm water and begin to carefully walk it back. As hard as I try most of the water spills out along the way.

"Marion, there is hardly any water here. Next time Carolee will fill my basin." I am never chosen again.

Who cares anyway. I look forward to going home to 11 Metropolitan Oval and playing with my friends.

There is Natalie Papnos in 2E. Her dad is a police officer and her mother wears big platform shoes made out of straw. All goes well playing at her house until they give me a sesame candy and my mouth and throat swell up, bad! I run out and take the stairs two at a time to the fourth floor.

My mother sees my swollen face and immediately calls our lady doctor, Amelia Fibus, who arrives in minutes with her black bag and the life-saving shot of adrenalin.

Next, I love Sandra Kohl. She lives in 2B. She has a nasty little brother who we always lockout of her room. We have read somewhere that there is a magical smell that emanates from the inside of a cracked drum. With our fists we smash open her brother's favorite toy drum. There is no smell, but her loudmouth mother comes banging on the door.

"What are you girls doing in there. Open the door this minute!"

We open it and I go running out.

"I'm sorry, I'm sorry."

"Come here this minute you little brat."

I have reached the front door.

"I hate you!" I scream and slam out as fast as I can.

I am a bad girl.

Then we have Carol Smarz. Her house is the "touch nothing" palace.

Unlike my 50's modern furniture, she has very fancy French. Her mother yells at her a lot and sometimes hits. We must stay in her room and so we play carefully with her porcelain headed dolls. We love to look under the dresses and into the underwear of each doll in hopes of seeing something important. We also love poking their eyes with pencils. We're looking to see a brain, but really we just like being naughty.

Most fun of all is Judah Judell. He lives in 3B, right under my apartment. He has very strict German parents who make him practice *Fleur-de-lis* on the piano every single evening at dinner time. We can hear it loud and clear. Like Pavlov's dogs we know it's time to eat.

Judah is extraordinarily thin, with extra skin like a snake. Judah's greatest talent is his ability to pull his knee and elbow skin way out, far beyond any human being. He demonstrates his skin pulling ability whenever he has an audience. We children all congregate at the little playground outside our apartment building. We look forward to seeing Judah's skin pulling act and beg for more.

"Judah, how do you do that?"

"I want to try it!" We have little success.

One day Judah falls off the monkey bars and skins both his knees and one elbow. No one wants to see, but we can't resist looking at the horrible bloody skin that hangs there. We all help to drag him home. We take him up the elevator to his apartment and ring the doorbell.

"Vat have you done to my boy?" Mrs. Judell screams in a heavy German accent.

"He fell Mrs. Judell."

Mrs. Judell grabs Judah by the collar with one hand and pulls him into the apartment. With her other hand, she slams the door in our faces.

We hear more screaming, crying and hitting. He does not appear outside for over a week. When he does, he is a changed boy. He remains subdued and does not participate in play activities. His elbow and knees are wrapped in white bandages. In the evenings now we only hear his mother screaming and hitting him. We do not hear *Fleur de lis* for two more weeks.

I love my friends.

The Best Thing I Ever Ate

"Marion, daddy is almost finished making the cardboard microphone for your birthday party."

I am so excited about my upcoming 5th birthday. It is1943. All my friends and cousins are invited. Dad is making a facsimile of the 1940s, round, stand up, radio mic so everyone can sing into it.

"But remember Marion, with your cow's milk allergy, you'll have to eat your goat milk junket, while the others are eating ice cream."

"Mommy, when can I drink regular milk again?"

"We'll try it next year and see what happens."

The party is all I hope for until the cake and ice cream. We love wearing party hats, playing pin the tail on the donkey, dancing to 78 RPM records, blowing into our noisemakers and singing in front of Dad's perfect microphone.

Mom claps her hands, "Back to the table everyone. Time for birthday cake and ice cream. Marion, make a wish and blow out the candles." I look happy. *But I wish I didn't have to eat that disgusting goat milk junket.*

Everyone gets a heaping bowl of vanilla ice cream with chocolate sauce, which I am also allergic to. I get the beige-colored, gelatinous, mucousy Junket.

Cousin Philly, sitting next to me opens his mouth wide for a huge spoon full of ice cream. He skims off the top, as he slips the spoon back out. There is still a nice mound of ice cream. He repeats the action. I am so jealous.

Philly looks down at my bowl and yells for all to hear.

"What is that? It looks like vomit!" Everyone is staring and laughing.

Hot and red in the face I scream, pointing at Mom and Dad, "They make me eat this!"

Humiliated I push the bowl away. Mom comes running over to place a big piece of cake in front of me. I try to control my tears. The party resumes.

I do not have to wait a whole year. One day, we hear the Good Humor man's jingle bells.

"Let's give it a try, Marion. I think you'll be okay."

Mom and I run over to greet him. The Good Humor man, in his clean white uniform, gives me a vanilla ice cream dixie cup with a little wooden paddle. I slowly peel open the lid. I can smell the vanilla. I can see the tiny dots of vanilla beans. My mouth waters. I dip the flat spoon in and take my first bite. I feel the sweet, cool, creamy pleasure on my tongue. I taste the real vanilla.

It is the best thing I ever ate!

Amazingly, there are no more hives, no more eczema, no more gagging or choking. I still can't eat nuts, but am able to begin my delectable, milky, culinary journey. Not least will be my delight in all the ice cream, flans, cheesecakes, homemade chocolate puddings and milkshakes that I will consume. Junket is banished.

One of my favorites is grilled cheese. Mom butters the insides and outsides of white bread and sandwiches in two slices of American cheese. The aroma as it fries stimulates my taste buds. My mouth waters. Finally, I eat the crunchy, gooey sandwich, slowly appreciating every bite.

"Mom, this is the best thing I ever ate."

With time, I can not decide on my favorites. Made from scratch Mac and Cheese? Or perhaps baked potatoes made in the dome-shaped baker? This potato is crunchy on the outside and steamy and soft inside. The potato is mashed and drips with butter. It is topped with shredded cheddar and a glob of sour cream.

This is surely the best thing I ever ate.

Nowadays, I still enjoy delicious food. But never again will anything taste as good as that first spoon of Good Humor vanilla ice cream.

It is the best thing I ever ate.

Please Let Me Die

Baskets of fruit and vegetables sit on the kitchen counter next to what appears to be two parts of a juicer; a grinder and a press. These are the components of the latest 1945 model. I am thinking we are the only family in the Bronx to own such a contraption.

Friends are always saying, "What is that thing?"

"I'm not sure, I think it's my Dad's juicer."

I am embarrassed.

The refrigerator is stocked with salad greens, fresh spinach, broccoli, eggplant, soy milk, yogurt, whole-grain loaves of bread and a jar of Kretchmer Wheat Germ. Cabinets above contain packages of brown rice, whole grain crackers, dry fruit and a bottle of Black Strap Molasses. In 1946 my father is of the belief that eating healthy, drinking home pressed juices and taking supplements will prevent him from getting cancer. Mother is of the same mind but has insisted that we include fresh meats and dairy products in our diet. We listen to nutritionist Carlton Fredricks on the radio and treat ourselves to lunches at Vim and Vigor Restaurant on 57th Street.

"Dad, can't we go to the Horn and Hardart Automat? I love their Mac and Cheese."

"Well, maybe next time Marion. Vim and Vigor is healthier."

As an eight-year-old child, I help make the juice. I love to cut up apples, carrots, strawberries, and celery for Dad to grind. I watch him remove the pulp onto a large piece of cheesecloth which he folds and places on the press. As he presses down hard, I am fascinated as I watch the orangey colored juice pour into each glass. I sip with mild satisfaction but secretly wish for a milkshake and an Oreo cookie.

In third grade, I am reading and practicing the Zana Blouser method of writing. I am learning about Eskimos and doing arithmetic. Mostly I like drawing igloos, bears, and walruses.

I like my friends a lot. On weekends my friends come over and Dad shows eight-millimeter movies of Charlie Chaplin and the Three Stooges.

In particular, I like my friend Stevie Brown. Sometimes we play board games after school at my house. My mother makes our popcorn.

When Stevie Brown's father invites my dad and me to a puppet show in Manhattan, I am thrilled. We are to travel on Saturday to a 2:00 p.m. show in their brand new Studebaker. It is white with brown leather seats. They will pick us up at 1:00 p.m. Mom emphasizes my need to eat a good lunch before we go. She prepares a leftover veal cutlet, a baked potato, and some lovely cooked spinach.

I finish most of it. I am a good girl.

The car is truly beautiful, shiny and new, the inside smells of leather. Dad and I sit in the back where the leathery smell brings on mild nausea.

The Bronx scenes whiz by, Bruckner Boulevard, the Willis Avenue Bridge. I look out of the window at the blur.

I am feeling somewhat dizzy now and try to close my eyes. My vestibular system has always hated the back seat and I begin to feel woozy. I open my eyes and close them again trying to concentrate on pleasant things.....No, don't think about food, flowers, maybe....no, the thought of their aroma adds to the queasiness.

We are halfway there.

"Just hold on," I pray. My hands are sweaty and clenched tightly in my lap. I start to take deep breaths.

"Just breathe," I think, "and you'll feel better."

"Dear God please let us be there soon. Please let me make it."

I breathe more deeply, I am hyperventilating, my fingers are numb and tingly. I feel the color draining from my face. The friendly chatter around me is only a buzz in my head. We must almost be there now. I see the Manhattan streets gliding by. Now my face is sweating and my hands are ice cold. I know what is coming. There is no stopping it now.

The sickness comes with a loud retching sound. It pours out at once all over my coat into my lap, over the seat and floor mat. It has the consistency of oatmeal and is spinach green. The odor is immediately discernible and everyone shrieks.

We pull over to the curb. Everyone is yelling with fierce black angry mouths. Dad yanks me out of the car, barking something.

I am sobbing. Dad rips my coat off and throws it in a garbage bin. Stevie and his dad are screaming at me as they find paper towels and seltzer water in the trunk. They throw the floor mat in the trash and furiously start cleaning the back seat. I am shivering and crying.

There is no sympathy.

"Why didn't you tell us you felt sick? My car is ruined!"

"What is wrong with you?"

"I'm so sorry!" I scream. "I thought I could wait." People on the street are stopping to stare.

I am such a bad girl.

We do go to the puppet show. I have no memory of it. We drive home in silence. A blanket has been thrown over the place where I sit. Stevie Brown never speaks to me again.

Please Let Me Die!

Good Girl/Bad Girl, Part One

How is it I wonder, that a sweet, curly-haired, cherry-cheeked little girl wants to do naughty things? For her first decade, she obeys mommy and daddy. She wants to please them, but now she just as much wants to please her friends.

A dilemma.

And what interesting and naughty friends she has.

I am not sure when life begins to change. Sixth grade is going well. I get good grades and take piano lessons. That I am terrible at playing the piano is an understatement. But walking the fifteen blocks to school every day with my close friends and hanging out with them is what I live for.

It is springtime when Betty Keller moves into the apartment next to mine and the trouble begins. She is a blond-haired, pale-skinned, eleven-year-old, an only child like myself. She takes a liking to me and we start to walk home from school together.

Her father travels a lot and her mom works, as do mine. We both have keys to our apartments and often visit with each other until our mothers get home.

One day, at my house, we roast marshmallows over the stove. We cook spaghetti and light candles. When a roll of paper towels catches on fire, we are screaming hysterically,

"Throw it in the sink! Pour water on it! "

"Sparks are sticking to my sweater!" Betty screams.

I am beating Betty with a wooden spoon. Now there are little black holes in her sweater. She will have to throw the sweater out.

When my mother gets home, she can smell the remains of the fire and forbids us to ever use the stove again.

Unlike my mother and father, Betty's mom and dad smoke cigarettes and drink alcohol. One day at her house we decide to pretend to smoke with drinking straws. We use the stove, once again, to light the tips. As we breathe in the smoke we start to gag and choke, our throats are burning.

"We should try real cigarettes." Betty chokes. "I can get some of my Dad's Lucky Strikes. But we can't do it in the house."

"Ok," I say delighted.

"I know where he leaves his car keys when he's traveling. We can smoke in his car." she giggles.

I am on my way to becoming a bad girl.

Betty's dad parks his Buick sedan on the top outdoor level of the neighborhood parking garage. We meet the next day after school and walk the two blocks to the garage. As we skip along, I ask, "Betty, what's in the bag?"

"It's a surprise."

I grab the crumpled bag and run ahead. I open it and peek in to see an amber bottle half full with brown liquid.

"What is this?"

"Don't you know what Canadian Club is? You are so dumb."

We enter the garage and are pleased to see that no one is around. We ride the elevator to the top floor.

We settle into the front seat of the big comfortable Buick and Betty lights a cigarette. She seems to know what she is doing.

"You have to inhale to enjoy it," she says.

I light one up and gently puff it.

"You are so wimpy!" she laughs. Betty is screwing off the top of the half-full amber bottle. She takes a gulp with a loud exhale.

"Aaaah. Now you try it."

"I don't know. I never did this before." But how can I refuse? I bring the bottle to my lips, take a sip and swallow. It burns my throat but begins to warm as it works its way down. We are now smoking and drinking and laughing hysterically.

I am such a bad girl.

As it begins to get dark, I realize that my mother will be home soon.

"Let's go!" I yell.

Betty locks up the car and we scramble down the steps. No time to wait for the elevator.

We stagger down the street and scream and laugh with sheer abandon.

"Oh God, please don't let mom be home yet." I pray.

I am dizzy and shake as I turn the key in the lock of the front door. I have gotten home in time to take a shower, brush my teeth and get into bed.

When mom comes home and finds me she wonders if I am sick.

"I will bring you some soup," she says.

"No, mom, that's ok, I'm just tired, I want to go to sleep." And I do.

I am a very bad girl.

Good Girl/Bad Girl, Part Two

Betty Keller and I were only eleven when our adventures first began. It is now the summer and we are twelve. Like a good girl, I obey Mom and go to dreaded day camp for four weeks. But now, for the rest of the summer, Betty and I are on our own to explore the neighborhood on bikes, roller skates and on foot.

Our Bronx neighborhood, Parkchester, has a busy shopping area. This includes a Lowes American movie theater, specialty shops, Woolworth's and Macy's. Our parents work so we are latch key kids. How thrilling to go off each day into a safe world, never knowing what will happen next.

It starts slowly by pinching money from our mom's drawers and purses. We walk to Woolworths, buy little note pads and pens, balloons and greeting cards. At lunchtime, we meander to the store's long lunch counter to eat hamburgers or grilled cheese. We giggle with delight as we order the biggest, super-duper, black and white ice cream sodas for dessert. We are free to do as we please. Betty always plans ahead for the next day.

"Why should we always take money from our moms? They are bound to find out, right? It would be so easy to just take a few little things from, maybe, Macy's." A shiver runs up my spine at the contemplation of actually stealing things.

"I don't know, I'd be too scared. What if we get caught?"

"We won't get caught. You are such a wimpy kid, Marion."

Macy's is the Mecca of merchandise. In summer it is always cool inside with a vague perfume aroma emanating from the cosmetics department. Stately mannequins pose for us wearing the top styles of the day. Counter displays are artistically arranged for all to see and touch. Scarves, gloves, wallets, shirts, and sweaters are there for purchase. We are especially attracted to the jewelry counters. There, earrings, bracelets, and necklaces hang and glitter from racks, all to be fondled by the customers.

Most exciting is the large tray of scatter pins, the hot items of the day. They are to be worn on sweaters and blouses in varying arrangements. Girls collect them and wear them with pride pinned toward one shoulder, beneath fake peter pan collars. The tiny enamel flowers, kittens, frogys, and rhinestone sea horses sparkle and glisten, asking to be caressed.

Betty does it first. The plan is to casually touch each pin as we have been doing. Then as I make clear that my handling is all above counter, with no one looking, she slips one into her pocket. Slowly, in a relaxed manner, we execute our plan, then move on to other parts of the store. OMG, it is so easy. Our plan is carried out to perfection. On the street again we howl with laughter, thrilled to have pulled it off.

We wait several days and notice a new sales clerk before we try it again. Now it is my turn. I have particularly fallen in love with a shiny, jewel-encrusted, green and red parrot. My hand shakes with fear as I try to act natural. The salesgirl is turned away helping a customer. As part of the plan, with Betty chatting nonstop, I clumsily grab the pin and put it in my pocket.

"Stay calm," Betty admonishes, "Just walk slowly." I can feel the hot breath of the store manager on my neck. But no, there is no one. It seems like forever before we get outside into the steamy August day. I shake but I am exhilarated.

I am such a bad girl.

Why does this feel so good? Is it the danger? Fear of getting caught? Is it a desire to rebel against parental control? Is it the thrill of getting something for nothing?

Who knows?

When Mom finds out that I'd been stealing money from her purse the grounding seems fair and the summer is over.

I promise to be a good girl.

First Date

September brings what had fearfully been anticipated, attendance at a new school, junior high PS 36. I am twelve-years-old, in seventh grade. It is 1951. We are required to purchase passes to the public bus and get to school on time every day. Getting home leaves room for flexibility.

I meet Edwina Nordgren in math class. I envy her straight blond hair and blue eyes. This is topped off by the fact that she is brilliant at math. Her seat is right next to mine and she often lets me copy her answers. We start to hang out together on the concrete play area at recess. It is easy to slip away and cross the street to the neighborhood candy store where we buy two-cent egg creams and five-cent ice cream cones. My favorite flavor is coffee. As long as we return in time to line up, it works.

Edwina has a boyfriend, Marty Strauss. She tells me that they often go to her house, a World War II Quonset hut, after school, where they smoke cigarettes and make out. Make out?

"What do you exactly mean?"

"Well, we just kiss a lot."

Edwina wants to fix me up with Richard Peroni. He is a very cute dark-haired boy with a perpetual tan.

"Richie likes you. He says he wants to go out with you."

"He does?"

"Yeah, the four of us can go to the movies on Saturday. Want to?"

"I guess so, I don't know him too well. He's so cute, why not?"

I agree to the movie date for the four of us. We meet at the Lowes American in Parkchester. I wear my best yellow sweater. Toward the upper left shoulder there shines the parrot scatter pin I shoplifted from Macy's. Richie, who looks very handsome, wears a nicely ironed white shirt. He vaguely smells of Canoe aftershave lotion. Wait a minute, how could that smooth-faced boy actually be shaving? No matter.

The boys have already bought the four twenty-five cent tickets. So sweet.

We find back row seats in the smoking section. Edwina has a pack of Marlboro's that we think we can share. I never smoked again after trying it with Betty Keller so I am anxious. Lucky for me, the movie matron immediately comes by and tells us to move to non-smoking. She is a witch of a woman, with an old lady perm. She wears a brown uniform and orthopedic shoes. Her weapon is her flashlight, which she uses indiscriminately to probe the goings-on of the teenaged members of the audience.

Apparently, the boys have devised a plan, because at a given cough signal they both put their arms on the back of my and Edwina's seats. A few minutes later the arms drift to our shoulders. After a while Richie's hand begins to hang down past my parrot scatter pin, hovering tenuously above what one day will be a breast. This makes me very nervous and I begin to squirm. He takes the hint and retreats.

A few minutes later and another cough the boys both turn their heads toward each of us for a kiss. I understand what I am supposed to do but am not eager. We bump noses as we kiss lightly. I can smell the garlic on Richie's breath.

This is not for me. I jump out of my seat.

"Hey, where are you going, Marion?"

"I have to go to the bathroom. Anyone want candy? I'll get some."

Edwina laughs hysterically.

"Get Goobers and Raisinettes."

"Ok."

I wait several minutes in the bathroom, trying to figure out what to do or say. I have no money so I can't buy candy.

When I finally head back, from the rear I can see Edwina and Marty making out. Richie just sits there with his arms folded. When I slide into my seat I can tell that he feels hurt. He barely speaks to me afterward when we leave to buy ice cream.

So much for my first date.

I Have That

When Woody Allen was asked to write a few words about his hypochondria he balked.

"I am not a hypochondriac, but actually a totally different genus of a crackpot. I am an alarmist." Here is the difference.

He wrote, "I don't experience imaginary maladies. My maladies are real."

What distinguishes his hysteria is that at the appearance of a mild symptom he concludes he is dying. This leads to many visits to the Emergency Room. When I see this piece in the New York Times I perk up.

"That's me!"

But wait. I am not only an alarmist, but I am a hypochondriac too. When I empathize with my friends I can feel their pain, the dizziness, the weakness, the palpitations, and the lumps.

I have examined my history in order to discover where this syndrome began and how it evolved. As an only child of very loving, hovering parents it began early. We lived in apartment 4B in the newly built apartment complex in the Bronx called Parkchester. It was a safe paradise for families. It had beautiful parks with play and recreation areas for children. Everyone looked out for each other. There were always kids to play within the building. I loved riding the elevator to my friends' apartments. I remember how independent I felt at age seven.

One day I am playing with Natalie Padnos in apartment 2D. They ask me to stay for dinner and offer a sesame candy for dessert. Almost immediately after swallowing it my throat and lips begin to swell. Then come the pain and choking.

"I don't feel so good!"

"Marion, your face is all red and your lips are swollen."

I slam out and run up the stairs crying hysterically.

"Mommy, I can't breathe!"

Through my screaming and pointing, Mom understands that it is an allergy attack. The wrenching and vomiting help a bit, but I still can't breathe. Mom calls our doctor Emilia Fibus who shows up in minutes with her little black bag. She quickly administers a shot of adrenalin leaving me shaky and exhausted but it works. I begin to breathe normally. I learn that seemingly benign foods can become lethal poisons.

Kindergarten is a challenge. I love to play and learn things in school. Nevertheless, when I wake each morning to the enthusiastic voice of John Gambling on the radio show Rambling With Gambling coming from the kitchen, I begin to feel the dread, the sinking stomach, the fluttering heart, nausea. The oatmeal or cream of wheat at times will not stay down. Mom is always sympathetic. Dad not so much.

"Send her to school! There's nothing wrong with her. She's a hypochondriac!"

Sometimes Mom let me stay home. What fun we have. I draw pictures, we bake oatmeal raisin cookies and Mom reads me countless stories. My favorites are Dr. Seuss' *The Five Hundred Hats of Bartholomew Cubbins* and *Madeline*, by Ludwig Bemelmans. How perfect a story about a brave little girl's trip to the hospital.

I must confess I even enjoy some of my childhood illnesses. Within two years I have both measles and chickenpox which keep me in bed two weeks at a time. The coziness of the bed and the darkened room allow me to drift off to an imaginary universe. I love the bubbling, gurgling, glass-encased vaporizer. The inner workings look like a stone castle with turrets and windows. A valve spews up a lovely, faint eucalyptus smelling steam.

My mother brings chicken soup and Rice Krispies with milk, sometimes tea with lemon and honey. Best of all she sits next to me in a comfortable armchair and reads to me from the Water Baby Tales. I love the adventures of Tom the Waterbaby, all his friends and Mrs. Do-As-You-Would-Be-Done-By. It is only later that I learn that Tom was a dead child who came to live at the bottom of the sea after his death. Mom hid that information to protect me.

In high school I contract the "kissing disease." My alarmist tendencies reach full force. I come home from school in a hysterical state after finding two big lumps on either side of my neck. My throat is excruciatingly inflamed and I feel hot all over.

"Mom, I'm dying, I have cancer. I know it!" I howled.

She's great at bringing me down.

"Let's get you to the doctor and find out." A blood test confirms mononucleosis.

"Not much to do for this," says the doctor. "Take aspirin, drink lots of liquids and bed rest. You cannot go to school for three weeks because you can infect others. Not just by kissing."

"Three weeks, really? Not too bad."

Friends deliver my homework and I continue my lifelong journey and love affair with books. I read voraciously, *Of Human Bondage*, *The Great Gatsby*, *Wuthering Heights*, *Jane Eyre* and *Rebecca*. I became familiar with Eugene O'Neil's plays and I especially savor *Long Days Journey into Night*. The more depressing the better. No TV, no distractions, only radio and music. I take breaks to eat soft food, ice cream, soup, and sweet juices.

Even Dad is sympathetic; no accusations of hypochondria now. He brings flowers which he places in a vase in my room together with a big bag of lifesavers with every flavor.

Nowadays with modern health care, we alarmists and hypochondriacs do not fair well. A recent phone call to my doctor about some heart flutters is disastrous. The nurse finally calls back.

"Marion, I'm sorry, the doctor is away, so you have to go to the emergency room."

Many invasive tests and two thousand dollars later I am released with a diagnosis of nothing wrong.

I assume studies show that alarmists and hypochondriacs receive more medical care, but to what benefit? Do they live longer? Probably not. Who knows.

I'll be watching you, Woody Allen, to see how you fare.

Olfactory Factor

As a tiny child, I love to smell things. I love the smell of cooking food, of mint, of chocolate, of flowers, of grass. I love the smell of fresh linens, my chenille comforter and the smell of my mother and father. I love to fall asleep under my covers smelling the sleeve of my flannel pajamas. My father calls it my "snooze smeller."

I am conscious, too, of abhorrent odors. I have a vivid memory of Aunt Rella, my father's sister, who I only met a few times. She slept at our house one night and in the morning drew me into her arms under the bedclothes. I was suffocated by the stifling odor of her underarms. How sad, it is all I remember of her.

At home, I look forward to sniffing the fragrant meals my parents cook. So nice to have the appetite whetted by baking chicken and potatoes, grilled cheese and tomato soup, cookies, soufflés, and bread puddings. Pots bubble with stews and soups and eggs fry into tasty omelets. My appreciation for food and cooking begins very early in my parent's home.

At school, however, where lunch is served in the gym-cafeteria, I am nauseated by the horrible combination of tomato soup and peanut butter sandwiches, Lysol and children's sweat. I bring lunch but have a hard time swallowing as my nostrils sniff the putrid air.

As time goes on I become more and more conscious of the way people and animals smell. The Bronx Zoo, a favorite place to visit, is a lovely combination of sights, sounds and smells. I remember the camel and elephant rides, the monkey and lion houses and the wonderful seals, all croaking together at feeding time. I remember intimately the children's petting zoo, the soft furry lambs and bunnies, and their gamey smell. I remember, too, the awful allergy attack after all that petting.

"Mommy, I can't breathe. I'm choking."

"Quick, let's run to the water fountain. Here's a Benadryl. Drink it down and wash your hands and face!"

My mother was at the ready with the Benadryl she always carried for me.

She was good at keeping her cool too.

24

Best of all I remember the end of the day and the walk to the bus stop on my father's shoulders. I would lean forward to hold his head in my arms. He smelled clean with the vague remnant of aftershave.

Life becomes more complicated and my olfactory experiences increase. Among my favorites include the beach and ocean smells, hiking-in-the-woods smells, the restaurant smells and *Midnight in Paris* perfume. I particularly love the aroma of pizza parlors, bakeries, and Chinese restaurants.

Relationships deepen and strengthen as I begin to appreciate more and more the aroma of friends, family members, and boyfriends. By high school, I become more finicky. I am offended by bathroom odors, moldy smells, rotting food and human perspiration. There is a good healthy athletic perspiration and then there's the nervous sweat. Most of my friends, like I, become self-conscious of bodily odors and functions. We shower often and use deodorant. We brush our teeth and use mouthwash.

Even so, there are smells that distinguish one friend from another. Some smoke cigarettes and eat garlicky foods. Some refuse vegetables and salads for a steady diet of meat. Perhaps some inherit a particular family odor. I know, that I am either attracted or repelled by people based on fragrance.

Most interesting are the kissing experiences.

On a date, if we have imbibed in an evening of drinking beer or mixed drinks, breaths mingle and become quite pleasantly familiar. Good for kissing. Add to that pizza or spaghetti, not so much. In the long run, boyfriends can not conceal their true odor, nor perhaps can I. So the relationships that last are compatible olfactorily. This ultimately leads to my meeting Bob, my husband.

Now I will admit that there are moments when I question our olfactory compatibility, but for the most part, I love his scent.

He's an athlete, so there is a lot of clean athletic sweat.

We generally eat the same foods although he likes beer and I like wine.

He likes spicy and I bland.

So it usually works.

I believe that is why we chose each other in the first place.

Adolescence

It takes courage to grow up
and become who you really are.
— *EE Cummings*

The Kissing Game

My daughter Susie likes to hold my face in her tiny hands.
"Mommy, let's butterfly kiss." We are cheek to cheek as she
gently flutters her eyelashes against mine.
"Doesn't it tickle, mommy?"
"Yes, I love it! Let's do it again!"
My little boy, Jonathan holds my face and presses his lips to
my cheek.
"Hold still mommy, so I can kiss you." It is a long, sweet kiss.
Who can resist the purity of a child's kiss?

As a twelve-year-old budding adolescent, I am about to enter a
strange, exciting new world. My friends and I are curious about
everything. We have begun to break from the yoke of adult pro-
tection. We want to hang out in houses where parents don't lurk,
where we can be free and bad. A place to play kissing games.
At home I experience parental hugs and cheek kisses. Extended family, aunts and uncles, offer up messy smooches and
unwanted squeezes, making me cringe. In 1952 we know nothing
of what is to come later in the cyber age. We listen to beautiful
love songs and see adorable sex free movies. So kissing games
become the ultimate in pre-teen adventure.
Mostly we play spin-the-bottle. We use a classic Coke bottle
and spin it in hopes of getting someone good to kiss. There are
usually seven or eight boys and girls, none of whom I am anxious

to kiss, but I need the experience. Mitch Michaels is chubby with curly black hair. He has puffy, dry lips, not unpleasant to kiss. Mike Smith is cute, with a British accent. His kiss is wet which forces me to wipe my mouth with the back of my hand.

Mike asks me to go to the movies. I accept with trepidation and hate it when he holds my hand.

After an hour of torture, he says, "Boy, we both have such sweaty palms, don't we?"

"Yes, we do!"

He releases his grip and we both contentedly watch the movie.

Two of my good girlfriends play at these spin-the-bottle sessions.

There's Toby Z and Betty Cotton. What is unexpected is that Betty is in love with Toby and always tries to spin to her. Betty dresses like a boy, talks tough and loves girls. When she can't hang out with Toby, I become her second choice.

She is so much fun, so caring and generous, and a talented kisser. Unfortunately, Betty has to keep her sexual preference hidden. There is little tolerance for who she is in the fifties.

At age thirteen I am in eighth grade. Flirting at our junior high is comprised of smiling, bumping into someone you like and punches in the arm. Love words consist of

"Do you have the homework?"

"That teacher is a real jerk, right?"

I know Kenny likes me because he writes that I am his favorite kid in the class in my slam book. Everyone has a slam book where you keep records of kids' favorite things like colors, sports, friends, and foods.

I like Kenny too. I like his sick straight hair and blue eyes. Knowing Kenny likes me still leaves me bewildered because nothing happens.

It is not until the graduation dance in June that we actually speak and dance. Later, on this warm spring evening, Kenny walks me home. A light breeze blows as we meander along my tree-lined street. We are holding hands and quite gracefully stop to kiss. It is a warm, dry, perfect kiss.

Kenny moves to Kentucky the next week and I never see him again.

High school starts in 9th grade. Boy-girl relationships begin to change. Now there is real dating which includes going to the movies, out for pizza or ice cream and going to parties. The protocol is the boy calls the girl on the phone a proper few days before the Saturday date. Some people make the commitment to go steady, but most of us play the field.

Kissing becomes unique with a wide variety of individual differences. The boy becomes the leader and initiator.

I remember Robert Stackhouse who asks me out on a date. We have a fun time at the movies and out for a slice of pizza. He walks me home to my apartment building. He cordially rides the elevator with me to the fourth floor. We are awkwardly smiling but have nothing to say.

As we step into the hallway near apartment 4B Robert gently grabs my shoulders and presses me against the wall. He leans in for the kiss.

I'm thinking, "Okay I can do this."

Suddenly he thrusts his tongue into my mouth. He begins licking along my upper teeth as if to clean them. I pull away and he laughs. He is still pushing against me. I am unable to move. He takes my hand and roughly places it on the bulge in his pants. In a raspy voice, he says, "This is for you!"

"No, no, no, thanks!" I scream and push him hard.

"What the fuck!" He yells and runs down the four flights of stairs.

Monday back at school when Robert Stackhouse and I pass each other in the halls we turn away without so much as a nod.

Model Apartment

"You have to clean the toilet today, Marion."
"Why me, I'm the worst at it and I hate it the most."
"Tough cookies, Marion. It's your turn. You can't get out of it this time."

At P.S. 36 in the Bronx, as in every other junior high school in all the boroughs of New York City, girls in 8th grade have to take a class called Apartment. In the 1950's we are required to participate in this as part of a three-segment series that includes cooking and sewing. The boys have shop class learning to work with metal and wood, all year.

The wicked old-maid marm who teaches our class, has a wiry hair coming out of the mole on her chin. She is always dressed in black and is anorexically thin. This woman promises to prepare us for marriage.

This is accomplished by teaching us all the intricacies of cleaning an apartment. It includes lessons on the importance of cleanliness and the joys of neatness. I don't know how this teacher is able to dirty the apartment for each class meeting, but it is always a filthy mess, the bathroom especially grimy.

Of the three segments, I like cooking class best. I especially love putting huge globs of mayonnaise in the tuna fish, egg salad, and green Jello molds. None of which I ever have at home. The aroma of delicious chocolate chip cookies is followed by stuffing as many as we can into our mouths before the bell rings.

"Those are my cookies, I know the ones I baked."
"Yeah, yours all have weird shapes."
"Now girls, they all taste delicious."

I love the little mandarine oranges peeking out of cool whip ambrosia. We hate cleaning up there too, but we giggle hysterically as we all pitch in. Not so when it comes to Apartment.

The struggle to master the treadle sewing machine is almost as bad. Thread keeps getting stuck and the stitching is always crooked. It is impossible to get the rhythm of your feet on the treadle and the push-pull of the wheel all at the same time. We have to make jumpers in preparation for making our own graduation dresses. Mine is a not-too-ugly, green waffle-patterned cotton that hangs crookedly, with lumpy pockets and twisted bodice. My girlfriends and I decide to wear our jumpers on the same day and suffer the raucous laughter of the boys.

When it comes to the graduation dress I am at a complete loss. Mom buys me a few yards of beautiful white piquet material and helps cut out the pattern. The actual sewing is another thing entirely. I end up with a torn, gathered up mess. Fortunately, when I come home crying, my mother takes me and the dress upstairs to 5B to Mrs. Becker, the seamstress. At times like this, I really appreciate living in our apartment in Parkchester. Our building holds the wonders and talents of a hundred people.

"Oh boy, this is quite a challenge. But don't worry I can fix it."

She tears the dress apart, pins me up with what's left of the soft white cloth. In two days she makes me a lovely, capped sleeved graduation dress. I proudly wear it on graduation day with several crinolines and feel gorgeous.

Back to the Apartment.

In the beginning, I have no idea what "Apartment" is. It is in the basement of the building down a dark sinister hallway. It has an old dingy door that creaks when it opens. We are always frightened to enter, tiptoeing in the dim light. You are assigned to "Apartment" with nine other girls in order to learn how to clean house, make beds, iron and properly dress.

On the first day, our old, stiff-necked teacher lectures us about how important it is, when dressing, to put your skirt on first and then your freshly ironed blouse, which has been on a hanger. After the skirt is on you can undo it and tuck in the blouse very carefully. We are all choking and gagging to squelch our laughter. A demerit here can mean detention.

I am dying to know if the curriculum was exactly the same in as far away as Brooklyn.

Each time we meet in the "Apartment" we have to decide among the group who will team up for the kitchen, bedrooms (hospital corners), living room, closets, and bathroom. Who will Hoover and who will dust? Somehow there are always old clothes in the closets, plenty of dust and dirty dishes in the sink. Did someone actually live here?

You never wanted to get the bathroom with its rusty faucets and rank odor. In the corner stands a plunger to be used every time, for the stuffed toilet, bathtub, and sink. Why are there always wads of hair stuck in the drains? Who actually uses this bathroom? Perhaps our teacher?

An old gray mop is used with Ajax cleanser for the floor. Old rags are used for everything else, of course, with Ajax.

Lucky for me I have one good, chubby little friend who I can bribe to do my bathroom duty.

"Sandy, if you do it today, I will take you to the candy store after school."

"I don't know Marion, you only got me an egg cream, a pretzel, and three marshmallow twists last time."

"How about I add four chocolate jelly rings and a coffee ice cream cone?" I calculate it will all come to fifteen cents. Well worth it.

"Ok, Marion, but don't ask me ever again, or else I'll tell on you."

We have come a long way, baby! Can you imagine our daughters ever actually taking a course in house cleaning?

It makes me feel very old to think that we were segregated and subjugated in that way without complaining. We did have an inkling that this was ridiculous, causing lots of joking and laughter.

We wondered too, what went on in the awesome, brightly lit woodshop where boys made birdhouses and bookshelves, and sometimes came away with bloodied fingers. They would show their wooden objects and war wounds with pride.

We never even thought to ask if we could try it.

Which Twin Has the Toni?

I have bleached, dyed, colored, and highlighted my hair. I have curled, straightened and ironed my hair. I have used curlers, bobby pins, large rollers, and small rollers to tame my hair. I have cut, shaped, teased, twisted and braided my hair. I have tried conditioner, mousse, gel, gloss and hair spray.

I am always searching for the perfect me.

I have lived through ever-changing hair fashion. I am born when Eleanor Roosevelt sports the fly-away bun. I live through the Mamie Eisenhower bangs, Jackie Kennedy bouffant, the Lady Bird flip and the Nancy Reagan study in perfection.

I am always searching for the perfect me.

In the early 1950's my favorite retail store in Parkchester, the Bronx, after Macy's, is Woolworths. There, you can find products with the most appealing and appalling advertising. "Headache and exhaustion? Drink Coca-Cola"

"Drink Coffee, you can sleep when you're dead."

An Ex-Lax spin-off, "Laxette, Laxative for Children, Yummy going down" Not so coming out.

Hard to believe is, "Eat, Eat, Eat, Stay Thin with Sanitized Tapeworms."

I love hair products like, "Penetrator Hair Brush brushes every strand" or "Suave your Hair with Helene Curtis."

Most of all I love Toni permanent wave cream, "Which Twin Has the Toni?" The whole country is attempting to guess at this game. Twin girls appear on the box, on black and white TV and in newspapers. You can not tell their hair apart. Amazing.

Woolworths, to my delight, offers, besides its soda fountain and delicious food bar, free demonstrations. I stand mesmerized as a sales representative rubs black liquid tar onto a piece of carpeting. An audience gathers to watch as the rep pours cleaning fluid onto a cloth and miraculously completely cleans away the abhorrent goo. Wow!

Naturally, I am drawn to demonstrations of hair products. The best one displays a fake wig on a stand. The sales representative points to the dull brown, frizzy, tangled mass of hair. The rep, with rubber-gloved hands, saturates the hair with the new foamy, experimental product and starts to brush the wig with gusto. What emerges after hundreds of strokes and help from a hand-held hairdryer is a golden, lustrous, perfectly wavy head of hair.

I am transfixed. I want that. The product is called "Perfect You."

I purchase the pint-sized brown bottle.

At fourteen years old I am on my way to the perfect me.

I secretly bring the hair product home and hide it in a drawer until I am alone in the house. I read the warning label.

"This product may cause unexpected changes in hair. Patent Pending."

Finally alone one day after school, I go into the bathroom, put a towel around my shoulders and begin. I take the rubber band out of my long, curly, dirty blond ponytail. I shake my hair loose. I cannot find rubber gloves so I proceed anyway. I shake the bottle as directed. I screw off the cap and am taken aback by the pungent, medicinal odor, something like the peroxide mom puts on cuts. Thick foam bubbles out of the bottle. I saturate all of my hair until the bottle is empty.

Oh, God, my hands are burning, on fire, and they turn red. I quickly soap them up and rinse. Patting my hands dry with a towel I wait for the miracle hair transformation.

After two minutes I feel the blazing burn.

After five minutes I am in agony. I look in the mirror and see a green tinge to my hair. I start to brush and clumps of hair come out.

"Help me God!" I scream. I jump into the shower and wash my hair over and over again with shampoo. When I emerge and towel-dry my hair I look in the mirror and find to my horror chunks of greenish-brown hair missing.

I am crying hysterically when my mother suddenly appears. She has come home early from work.

"What is going on here? What are you doing? What did you do to your beautiful hair?"

"Mom," I scream, "I can't believe I did this. I saw it at Woolworths and it looked so perfect in the demonstration, what should I do now? I can never go out again, what if someone sees me?"

I am covering my hair with a kerchief as my mother calls the beauty parlor down the street for an appointment.

I walk arm in arm with mom, my head down, crying as we enter the shop. The beautician leads me to a secluded corner of the shop and starts to cut.

When she is finished, I look in the mirror and see my new, soft, light brown poodle cut. I like it.

I have found the perfect me.

Teen Years

When you are a teenager you are
   experiencing things for the first time.
Teen stories are beginnings. — *Anonymous*

Send this Child to Camp

The advertisement reads: "Fun activities, water sports
on beautiful Kiamesha Lake, in the green rolling hills of the Catskill Mountains." It continues: "Nurturing staff, delicious food, a
perfect camp experience at Camp Na-Sho-Pa."

In 1953, at age thirteen, an only child, I have avoided the dreaded
possibility of going to sleep-away camp.
   Now, Mom points out,
   "You have the opportunity to see what it's all about as a CIT,
a Counselor In Training." I relent.

The camp bus picks us up at a designated spot in Manhattan. I
am already sick to my stomach and am happy to have taken Dramamine for the trip. As I scan the crowd of joyously screaming
kids, I realize that I am alone. I search for another terrified and
forlorn face. It is then that I see a tall, blond-haired girl, with rather
pleasing, irregular features and full lips.
   I approach and say, "Is this your first year?"
   Her face relaxes and she grins, "Yes, is it yours?"
   "Yes," I laugh. "Do you want to sit together on the bus?"
   "Yes, of course!". I introduce myself. Her name is Brenda.
   The four-hour trip passes pleasantly.
   Brenda and I have a lot in common so we chat away and doze
off every now and then. Finally, we drive onto a dirt road in a

wooded area. The bus emerges into an open space lined with rows of cabins and a large main house, the dining hall. The dinginess is apparent. The "beautiful" lake looks dirty brown.

There are two CIT cabins. As I enter mine the darkness of the one large room, with bunk beds and tiny windows, blots out the sunshine. There is an undeniable musty odor. I notice spider webs in the corners.

There are eight girls in each cabin. Here is my chance to get to know others.

In our cabin everyone is friendly, some having been to this camp before. One chubby dark-haired girl speaks up.

"Don't worry about the looks of this place, it's really fun. You stay busy all day with sports and arts and crafts and get to help the younger kids."

Another, anorexic-looking old-timer with skanky black hair says, "Stick with the mac and cheese at dinner, the mystery meat is really terrible."

A third pimply girl says, "Stay out of the lake unless you like swimming with frogs and snakes." Oh no. I am starting to get the picture.

I quickly become aware that the other CIT cabin has all the beautiful girls. It is clear that we are the plain, invisible group. Most of the gorgeous girls have been to Na-Sho-Pa forever and have found ways to shirk responsibility. They wear makeup, do their nails, and work on their hair. While the Plain Jane girls work hard at each sport and activity, the beauties take walks and relax. The staff begs them to get more involved to no avail.

In the evening after dinner, we have free time. We hang around outside the cabins talking about the boys whose cabins are not far away. One evening, as I sit alone on our front step, Lila, a lovely doe-eyed, Auburn, silky-haired beauty from the pretty cabin, comes over to introduce herself to me.

"How do you like it here so far?" she says.

"It's Ok but pretty boring." I think she will like me saying that. I want to impress her.

"Do you smoke?"

"Well, I've tried it lots of times." I lie.

"Do you know how to inhale?"

"Not really."

"Do you want me to show you how?"

"Sure."

"Let's go for a walk then."

You can not imagine how thrilled I am.

We take a nice long walk along a path lined with pine trees. Lila tells me that she is fourteen and from Long Island. Her parents make her come to this camp every year and she is used to it.

"The only bad thing is that I had a boyfriend last year. Do you know who Mike Meyer is?"

"Yes, he's gorgeous!" I say.

"Well, he dumped me and is going out with Stephanie." Another Miss America.

By now we are deep into the woods.

"Here's a cigarette. Just do what I tell you."

We light up and I begin to puff.

"You really never smoked. Right?" she says.

"Well, only a few times."

"Ok, you take a drag, and breathe it into your lungs."

She shows me in quite a professional way. The smoke comes out of her lips in a straight long stream.

My turn. I take a puff and inhale deeply, immediately choking. The horrible coughing fit lasts an eternity.

"You took too much in at once," she laughs.

We walk back talking all the way.

"I really like you," says Lila. "I think I can trust you. Let's take a walk tomorrow, ok?"

"Sure."

I am very happy.

Brenda is quite jealous of my new friendship with Lila.

"Why do you keep hanging out with Lila?"

"I don't know. You are still my best friend at camp. What was that idea you had?"

I don't know exactly how Brenda conjures up the idea, but we decide on a wicked and adventurous plan. It is halfway through the camp season and we are getting tired of the routine.

"Let's just get out of here for a day," says Brenda.

"You mean run away?"

"Yeah. Here we are in the midst of all these resort hotels. We can slip away after breakfast and head for the Concord."

"But how will we get there?"

"We can hitch rides."

"Do you think it's safe?"

"Sure, everyone does it."

"Ok."

The next day, after breakfast, we take some buttered rolls in a napkin, stuff them into our pockets with some money, and nonchalantly walk down the dirt road to the highway. It is easy to hitch rides with friendly people who direct us to the Concord Hotel.

This large, elaborate resort has everything. Beautiful swimming pools, chaise lounges, tennis courts, and a very green golf course. We ditch the buttered rolls and head for the luscious buffet. No one seems to notice us as we fill our plates. We eat lunch by the pool, relaxing, soaking in the sun and laughing with delight, wondering if the camp even knows we are gone. By 3 o'clock we know we have to go back.

This time, hitching rides isn't as easy and by the time we reach the dirt road to camp it is dark. We had hoped to sneak back without being noticed. So when we see the yellow camp bus coming toward us we quickly jump into the woods.

The bus comes to screeching halt just at the bush we are hiding behind.

"OK you girls, come on out."

The camp director yells more loudly than needed.

"What the hell did you think you were doing?" he screams. "We've been looking for you all day!" We slink out of the woods, heads down. Our faces, drained of color, are now red with shame and fear.

"We should kick you out, but first we are going to call your parents."

With profuse apologies and begging by us and from our parents, who cannot even begin to believe that we have done such a thing, the director finally gives in. We are permitted to finish out the weeks left in the summer.

By now the whole camp knows what we have done and very subtlety we become heroes. It is nothing overt, but we get lots of winks, high fives, and shoulder punches.

The girls in the pretty cabin actually greet us with smiles. Lila, in particular, gives me a quick hug every time I see her.

Although I never go back to camp Na-Sho-Pa, it is the best summer I have ever had.

A Bronx Kind of Innocence

To me, Parkchester was the most beautiful place on earth. I didn't know that people lived in single-family dwellings until I went to college. I grew up in the granite world of New York City.

Parkchester was different. It was a place where a *Parkie* was a cop who carried only a flashlight, where *Quad* was a quadrant which divided Parkchester into four sections. The *Oval* was a lovely wooded park with a large pool of goldfish and art deco fountains.

As children, we delighted in playing for hours with our pink Spaldings. Remember "A My Name?" We also used the pink balls to play punch ball with the boys. When our Spaldings wore out we would walk to the candy store next to the shoemaker with our friends for a new one. We rode our bikes and played Potsy. We jumped rope, mostly Connie One on Time. We roller-skated all over town, skate key around our necks.

In winter the snowplows came and created magical mountains in the parking lots. We dug tunnels and climbed up and slid down all day until we froze and went upstairs for a hot chocolate break.

At twelve years old we were allowed to take the bus to Pelham Parkway, transfer to the Bronx Zoo bus, and spend an entire day there. There were no killers, muggers or pedophiles. Later we took the same bus to Fordham Roller Rink carrying our boldly colored metal skate boxes. Our skirts had to be fingertip length.

We branched out to subway travel. I would board the elevated train at 177th and ride into the underground to the 92nd Street Y to take modern dance lessons. The occasional flasher was easy to avoid. It was not so easy to escape the subway guy who stood behind you as you grasped the strap above. He might press up against you in a rather questionable manner.

I became skilled at slipping away.

Subway travel continued throughout my years at James Monroe High School. Every day we walked the many blocks to the station, past the shops, the buildings with gargoyles, and Zaro's Bakery. By sixteen we had boyfriends and were seasoned enough on weekends to take the train to Wolman Memorial Ice Skating Rink, the MOMA or 42nd Street.

On Saturday night the girls would dress up in spiked heels, a straight skirt, a sweater with a neckerchief topped off with a *topper,* and we rode the train to Manhattan. The boys wore blazers and ties. We all hung on straps or leaned on poles and joked around. Sometimes we would walk from car to car to find the best one, no mean feat with three-inch heel shoes. We screamed with delight as we jumped over the windy gaps.

The biggest thrill was going to Birdland and Basin Street where we saw every jazz musician and singer from Louis Armstrong to Count Basie, Ella Fitzgerald, Thelonius Monk, Duke Ellington, and Dizzy Gillespie. We sat at tiny upfront tables for a small cover charge and the price of a few drinks, no questions asked. At sixteen we loved to order Canadian Club and ginger ale. We smoked cigarettes and crossed our legs in a sophisticated way.

The subway trip home was truly a joyride. Late at night the train was empty. Tipsy and giggly, we laughed the entire way, not one pervert or flasher in sight. Our heads would clear as we walked the long stretch from the station. Sometimes I took off my shoes and walked home in stockinged feet.

My parents, not sure exactly what we did, felt secure that we were safe at 1:00 am in Parkchester, the Bronx.

Humiliated

Sex is in the air.
Yet in the 1950s there seems to be little activity.

We have moved beyond the courting practices of Victorian times, the rebellious wild times of the twenties, and the austerity of the war years. We are post-war Americans, recovering, optimistic, powerful, and pleased with ourselves. The feminist movement and sexual freedom are yet to come. Never-the-less sex is in the air. It is just very difficult to actually experience it.

Keep in mind that women's contraceptives are impossible to come by. Girls have to wait until marriage to get a diaphragm from her doctor. The pill is nowhere on the horizon, which leaves condoms. The thought of even looking at one is anathema, a curse, to be reviled.

Boys, too, find condoms sinful. One can only purchase them from the pharmacist. Never are they found on the shelves A young man has to make the approach with cracking voice and shaking hands.

" A box of rubbers, please."

"What?" The clerk yells. "You don't even know what they're called, so you're not ready to buy them."

"But they're for my Dad." He is blushing furiously. By then, not only the pharmacist hears. A long line of customers is listening and giggling.

"Tell him to come back when he grows up!" someone says.

"When he's twenty-one!" another voice answers.

Why does he want them anyway if no one is doing it?

Wishful thinking? Bragging to his buddies? To keep one in his wallet just in case?

What does occur in the 50s is a beautiful and romantic ritual called dating. It consists of talking, flirting, phoning, joking, tickling, hugging, kissing, necking and best of all dancing. A few people in high school go steady, but most of us have dates with a variety of people of the opposite sex. We have tried out kissing

42

games, like spin the bottle, in junior high and are ready for the next step in high school.

This will often involve the boy calling the girl on Tuesday or Wednesday. Never on Friday, for a Saturday night date. The boy comes to the house to pick the girl up. Couples often go to a movie and out for pizza or ice cream.

In 1954, my favorite way to meet boys is at dances. We might connect in class but contact reaches its peak on the dance floor. Invariably there is a local band, playing the hits of the day.

The most exciting words girls wait to hear are, "Wanna dance?"

It is rude to say "No" to anyone and we girls suffer through torturous moments with sweet boys who have pimples, are clumsy, have smelly breaths or sweaty hands. Relieved when it's over, we always say "Thank you."

At one such dance, the moment I am waiting for actually occurs.

As a freshman, I have a crush on a boy who is a junior, an impossible dream. We have one class together. We are both in Orchestra, and we have chatted and flirted in the halls. His name is Mike Lewis. He has curly hair and sultry blue eyes.

On one particular Saturday evening in May, my friends and I attend a dance at the local synagogue. I dress appropriately in my favorite poodle skirt, two crinolines underneath, a sheer ruffled blouse worn over both a bra and lace camisole. I pin my ponytail into a sort of bun and dab Evening in Paris perfume behind each ear.

Suddenly, here he is, Mike, walking toward me. I look around thinking he is looking for someone else, but no, it is me.

"Wanna dance?"

"Sure."

His hands are dry and he smells faintly of Canoe aftershave. The first is a slow dance where we sway in perfect rhythm together. He gently places his cheek next to mine. We whirl, dip and sway some more.

Too soon it is over.

But he holds my hand and says, "Let's see what the next one is." It's a Cha-Cha. We are in lovely sync together, every step and turn in harmony. We dance and dance all night, Lindys,

Mambos and many slow ones. At the end of the evening, the band plays *Good Night Sweet Heart* and *Good Night Irene*. We all sing along.

Mike makes my life complete by saying, "Can I walk you home?"

It is a lovely spring evening and I live only blocks away. We walk and laugh holding hands all the way. At the door, we exchange the sweetest kiss.

"See you."

"See you."

I look forward to seeing Mike at school on Monday. In the hall he passes by and waves. At the beginning of class he waves but goes right to his seat. He seems somehow changed. After class he runs out.

What's going on? What did I do wrong? Why is he avoiding me?

Two days later I see him leaning over the water fountain and I tiptoe up to gently knee his rear.

I guess I kick a bit too hard because he turns around yelling "Shit, I'm bleeding." His teeth have knocked against the spout.

"Hey watch it," he sneers and walks away. I am devastated, humiliated and confused.

One of our friends, Joey from band class, is standing nearby observing it all. He walks over and puts his arm around me.

"I saw you at the dance the other night with Mike. Didn't you know that he's going steady with Sandy Giller? She was away for the weekend."

Of course, I didn't. I feel my face go red and hot tears well up. I run crying to the girls' bathroom.

Humiliated.

Redhead

I have always loved redheads. I find a special kind of beauty and vivacity in them. Strangely every time I meet up with a redhead there is an instantaneous connecting glint of attraction.

At James Monroe high school the redheads I knew were all male. I recall four in particular. Though not related they shared many similar characteristics: sensitive, funny, smart, talented and fragile.

There was Paul Brown, alcoholic, tearful, desperate for love and friendship.

At parties, Paul always cried,

"Marion, I'm so sorry, I just puked myself and you can smell it, I know you can. I have to stop drinking."

He died at age thirty in a car crash.

Then I remember Stu Marvin, the drummer. Short, talented, adorable.

"Marion, want to get high with me? We would have so much fun."

He died of a heroin overdose at twenty-five.

Next Eddie Z. He was one of my best friends. I remember, years later, his intervening in the "Baby Alive" family disagreement.

Susie, age five, whined, "I keep waiting for you to buy me a Baby Alive doll. All the kids have them. You can feed it baby food and then it poops. I want to call her Kathy. Please, please, it's almost my birthday. I love Baby Alive. I'll be so good, Mommy, please!!"

Daddy, as usual, is neutral.

My answer, "I find it totally disgusting that a doll can urinate, defecate and vomit. No, you cannot have that. Choose something else." I do not waver. I refuse to buy it for her.

But then along comes uncle Eddie who makes her dream come true. He shows up one day with the most beautiful, blond-haired, Baby Alive doll I have ever seen.

I demure and even help change its diaper. I insist on bathing it a lot, however. It is fun pouring scalding hot water down its throat to clean it up.

"Mommy, you're hurting my Baby Alive."

"It's all right, honey, we need to keep her clean."

Eddie never married. He had mysterious girlfriends, drank and smoked anything he could get and died at age forty-nine of lung cancer.

Now for number four. His name was Sid Philips.

Love comes to us in many ways and takes many shapes. It changes our lives, changes our personalities, and our expectations. It changes everything that will happen in the future.

Love can be so good and so bad.

Before I tell you more about Sid, I must digress for a moment.

Dancing was everything to me in high school. Everyone danced in the gym, at house parties, in dimly lit club rooms, and at sweet sixteen parties. The words, "Wanna dance?" evoked great excitement.

I remember the first actual ballroom dancing lessons I took at Arthur Murray's. It was in an upstairs loft on Tremont Avenue in the Bronx. I, along with a group of gawky thirteen-year-olds, was trying to learn to dance.

We didn't mind the dust on the floor, the shaky ballet bar or the soot-streaked windows. We just saw the tall gorgeous, Latin dance instructor, a touch of pomade in his wavy black hair. He always wore tight black pants and a fuchsia silk shirt open to the waist. We were lost forever.

"Now make a nice, wide line behind me and do what I do. Let's start with a Cha-Cha."

We all tried so hard to keep up with the Latin rhythms of Tito Puente.

"Okey guys, one-two, cha-cha-cha, one-two, cha-cha-cha."

His feet slid smoothly, hips swaying perfectly from side to side. We thumped and tripped behind him.

If he thought any of the girls showed promise, he'd ask her to the floor. While everyone watched, she would be swept around to foxtrot or waltz music by him, the God of dance.

I loved when he chose me. I didn't even mind that he often pressed the bulge in his tight black pants against my swirling poodle skirt.

All I wanted was to dance. Foxtrot, Cha-cha, Merengue, Samba, Mambo, Lindy, Stroll, even Waltz, Peabody, Polka, and Charleston, we danced to them all. We graduated with a Certificate of Dance. Everyone received one.

After all, we had paid our money.

Back to number four.

In the fifties, when sex was taboo, dancing took its place. Slow dancing was the all-time sexiest pastime, while fast dancing left us spent. I will never forget the night of the Halloween dance at the high school gym.

I am fifteen. The air our steaming high school gym is electrified. The music pulses loudly, hormones race. I along with the other girls hang out on the side, waiting for the sweetest words, "Wanna dance?"

The fear is that the short, chubby, sweaty-palmed boy who is plagued with early pattern baldness, will ask me to dance.

Why do they always pick me?

Suddenly a tall red-haired stranger appears before me.

Swooping down from nowhere he repeats the famous words "Wanna dance?"

He is at least six feet tall, broad-shouldered and handsome. His wide grin is infectious and his humor is stand-up quality. We move easily and perfectly together. Every spin, dip and turn is just right. We dance every dance effortlessly together for the rest of the night.

Abruptly, the strains of *Good Night Sweetheart* and *Good Night Irene* blare and everyone grabs their last dance partner. Singing loudly in unison, we end with *Don't Forget Who's Taking you Home*.

And he does. And he does for five more years.

Our relationship was long and complicated.

Fado Group singing about Lost Love

Sweet Sixteen

In 1955 the Sweet Sixteen party was the coming out for young women. It was not coming out as we know it today. In the Bronx, we were hardly debutants but still extremely excited at the prospect of this celebration. It had to include a special venue, a perfect dress, and an invitation list of the right boys and girls. Along with the excitement comes the fear, anxiety, and apprehension about getting it right.

Where to have it? What about food and music? Who to invite? Will anyone show up?

Many of my friends reach this fragile and challenging age before I do, so I get to study the process. Lucky are the boys of my generation who don't have to suffer this. They just have to show up in suits, dance, and eat. I check out my friends' parties, the restaurants, chicken dinners, fancy birthday cakes, and DJs. I study the tight bodices, full silky crinoline puffed dresses, and high heeled pumps.

There are hair, makeup, and undergarment issues. Some of my friends have started to wear panty girdles on their skinny bodies. One time I try one. We are out to dinner. The girdle is squeezing mercilessly into my stomach. I find the waiter.

"Excuse me, sir, where is the restroom?"

"The hallway to your left Miss."

I stumble down the hall feeling the food pushing up into my mouth. I can't breathe. I slam the stall door shut just in time. I rip at the layers of my crinolines to reach the girdle. With great effort I tear the truss halfway down with a sigh of relief. I can't remove it completely because it is holding up my stockings. I waddle back to the table feeling humiliated. The girdle and stockings have dipped to my thighs.

When my party time comes, I desperately want to be different.

So I decide to have it in our two-bedroom apartment, number 4B.

Let me help you picture it:

There is a nice long hallway that opens into a decent-sized eating area which is opposite the kitchen. Next, there is a big square living room with couch, piano, a few comfortable chairs, a coffee table and bookshelves, all in a modern fifties style. Then is an open door leading to a hallway and on the right is the bathroom.

Take a few more steps more and you are at my gray and red bedroom. My haven. It has a Castro-convertible sofa, a desk, two comfortable chairs, and a dresser with a mirror. The mirror is my favorite. It is large with a rectangular frame of hammered Mexican silver. It has sparkling, colorful pieces of glass woven throughout. I love bringing my friends to this room for teenage privacy and sharing.

Finally at the end of the hall is the master bedroom. Here, my co-operative parents are willing to take apart their double bed and place the mattress against the wall. This opens up a large space for dancing. The music is supplied by my 45-record player. We set up bridge chairs in the front hall and around the house.

My parents and I decide to serve a lovely spread consisting of fresh platters of deli meats which we call cold cuts. There will be roast beef, corned beef, turkey, tongue, and assorted cheeses. We will include freshly baked rye bread and rolls, and several nice fruit and veggie salads. There will be pickles, mayonnaise, mustard and Russian dressing in small glass dishes. Of course bowls of potato chips, Fritos and pretzels are scattered around. Guests will serve themselves on good paper plates and non-alcoholic drinks will be plentiful. Later there will be a beautiful, delicious, lemon-flavored four-tiered birthday cake with white frosting and pink and red flowers.

My mother and I shop for the perfect dress at Bloomingdales on 59th St. in Manhattan.

After an extensive search and much trying on, we decide on a champagne-colored, soft fiele, slightly low cut dress with cap sleeves. The skirt is not too full but still needs one crinoline. We dye silk shoes to match.

Next comes the guest list. This is a daunting task.

There are best friends, good friends, just friends, and acquaintances. There are the obligatory cousins and some next-door neighbors. I have a so-called boyfriend named Rusty Farrell who is at the top of the list. When the list reaches fifty we stop. I am sure that very few will come anyway so why not go all out?

My birthday is in December.

The special night arrives. The party is on a cold winter night and set to start at 8:00 p.m. By 7:30 I am losing control of my emotions and I am sure no one will come. By 7:45, I dry my tears, as some of my best girlfriends drift in. I am grateful.

Rusty shows up with two band members—a trumpeter and a piano player. He sets up his drums near the big picture window in the living room. Soon everyone is arriving and I usher them into various parts of the house. Friends place gifts on our small bridge table. Mom has set up a lovely food station in my bedroom, on the dresser, just like the one in the dining room to accommodate everyone.

My father starts taking the wonderful black and white photos he is famous for with his Argus camera. By 9 o'clock just about everyone has arrived and the party is beginning to pulsate. There is laughter, music, and dancing in the darkened back room and the little band is playing sweetly. That is the last I see of Rusty because he is too involved with making his own music.

Rusty on the left, Mel on the right

At 10 the doorbell rings. I run to answer the door thinking who can this be?

There stand five uninvited surly, delinquent boys. They sport leather jackets, turned up collars and greasy DA's. I know them from school. They are carrying two wrinkled paper bags.

"Hey, Marion, happy birthday, can we help you celebrate?" Oh boy, how can I say no?

"Sure, come on in. I'll show you around." As they slink in my Mom has a look of disdain but says nothing. I usher them to my bedroom where I tell them to make themselves comfortable. They immediately shut the door.

I return to the dimly lit back room to dance. We keep changing partners to strains of *Earth Angel, Go Have Your Fun Runaround, It's My Party* and *I'll Cry if I Want To*. We dance and sing loudly together. I love it. Things seem to be going well and I am happy.

Mom calls out that it's time to cut the birthday cake and sing Happy Birthday. As we all emerge to the dining area, I notice that the door to my room is still closed. Through the door, I can hear raucous laughter. The five boys do not come out to eat cake. By now Rusty and his band are playing loud, wonderful jazz. People are singing and clapping. The neighbors sit along the edges, eating cake and looking on with wonderment.

At 11:00 p.m. suddenly the doorbell rings several times. It is two local policemen. A neighbor has called to complain. They are very nice and just tell us to keep it down. We offer them cake, but they go on their way.

By 11:30 the party has quieted. Everyone is either sitting around or dancing slowly to subdued music. Yet there is still loud shouting coming from my bedroom. Without another moment's hesitation, my father yells for all to hear.

"What the hell is going on in that room?"

He walks briskly to the bedroom and bangs on the locked door.

"Open this damn door!" he roars.

Now there is complete silence throughout the house. The music stops, everyone turns to look. When he finally bursts through the door, Dad yells.

"Oh my God, You sons of bitches, get the hell out of this house."

The boys scurry past us, heads down, and run out the front door. Dad only permits Mom and me to enter the room. What meets our eyes is beyond comprehension.

Empty, dripping beer cans are strewn all over the room. Cigarette butts are stuck in the food. What food they have not eaten they have smeared all over my beautiful mirror and dresser. Designs are finger painted on the walls with mustard and mayonnaise. The furniture is askew. I cry in horror.

My parents tell me, "Marion, go back to your party, we will take care of this."

I try to regain my composure but am devastated and humiliated. Everyone starts asking me, "What's going on?" It takes all I have to appear composed.

"Those guys were drinking beer and made a mess."

Dad and Mom come out and she says, "No big deal, just continue as you were, but no one go into that room."

At midnight everyone starts to leave. There is a lot of kissing and hugging.

People keep saying, "This was the best Sweet Sixteen ever!"

Really??

Halloween Dance Photos, 1955

Marion on Sidney's shoulders

(L to r,) Marion, Iris, and Bunny

Senior Prom Photo, 1956

Sid & Marion

College

College friends become a kind of family.
You eat together, play and study together, fight,
laugh and cry together, do absolutely nothing
together until you can't remember how you ever
lived your life without them in the first place. —
Anon.

You Don't Know What Cold Is

The Cortland Gang after college

Our Cortland girl gang thought we knew what cold was
until December came. Cortland College is tucked away in the icy
north between Ithaca and Syracuse. We New York City girls
thought we knew it all, only to find out that there was another,
alien world out there.

The upstate college world.

Cortland was known as the *Phys Ed School.* Students often joked that it was not the soft drink, *Fizz Ed.* Fifty percent of the students were studying to be physical education teachers. The other fifty percent, my friends, were elementary education majors, a different breed.

There was one important exception. My cousin Marcia was the unique physical education major who was a beautiful and talented dancer. We were both lucky to belong to The Cortland Dance Group. Our instructor was Fanny, an accomplished dancer, and choreographer in the Martha Graham tradition. She worked us hard, taught us technique and choreography, helping us to choreograph and perform many of our own works.

In order to graduate, all freshmen had to take swimming. It was mandatory. No opting out. No medical excuse. No menstrual issues. No bad hair days. No sleeping late.

The Elementary Ed pool was in the basement of an old, off-campus, building. The pool water had an oily film. The old overhead pipes leaked rusty water. The floor was slimy with the Planters Wart virus.

The requirements were put to the test at the end of the semester.

1- Attend eight a.m. swim class twice a week, every week.

2- Tread water for five minutes. *I never treaded water in my life*

3- Execute four perfectly curved dives. Never flat. *I always just jumped in*

4- Swim the length of the pool back and forth for each of the three standard strokes: crawl, breaststroke, and sidestroke. They had to be kidding!

They were not kidding.

As freshmen, we saw no way out.

Attendance was taken every day by the buxom phys ed teacher, whistle around her neck, clipboard at the ready. She used a timer to clock our treading times. I drowned every try. It is impossible for me to stay above water. She laughs derisively at my attempts and blows her whistle when time is up.

Are you serious? I am at the bottom of the pool by then. I come up gasping for breath, begging for a reprieve.

"Do it again!" she yells.

When winter came the weather dipped to zero and below. Although we wore snow pants under our skirts, two sweaters and a sweatshirt over our blouses, heavy woolen mittens, a winter parka with a hood and fur-lined boots, we still froze.

Our hair froze too—into porcupine spikes. Our nose hairs stiffened making it hard to breathe. Every breath slashed at our lungs.

We trudged our way to our dorm at North Hall laughing and crying along the way. We had our girlfriends with us to help bear the pain. One girl on our floor had a bonnet hair dryer that we lined up to use. By the time it was my turn, my curly hair was a matted birds nest.

In December 1956, freshman year, I turned eighteen. It was the goal of all college girls to find a husband as soon as possible to start domestic life. A few years of teaching was more than acceptable. The aim was to attract a boy from Cornell or Syracuse in hopes of a permanent relationship.

On any given Saturday night lots of girls would line up along the second and third-floor balconies and along the banisters, hanging over the railing to wait for boys to come to Cortland looking for a date.

The boys in their camel hair Loden coats, with wood buttons, would look up to survey the pickings. They pointed to the one they liked. Often the girls breathed a sigh of relief if they weren't chosen and proceeded to play bridge, sing songs, tell funny stories and eat junk food.

One cold winter Saturday night six of us decided to put on our winter gear and trek down to The Tavern to check out the Cortland boys. They were like us, from nice working-class and professional families all striving to become great teachers. Many were from small cities and towns around the state. The new challenge was to keep up with the new level of drinking typical of Cortland students.

As you entered the Tavern a blast furnace smacked you in the face. The air was thick with the smell of whiskey and cigarette smoke. We tried to be cool as we stepped over the broken glass and headed for a table in the back. A drunk waiter approached.

"What'll it be? Vodka or beer?"

We all said beer although even that was strange to us. Soon Cortland boys came over to our table. We drank and shared where we were from and funny high school stories, laughing glee-fully. These were our kind of folk.

"I'm feeling tipsy," I whispered to my roommate.

"Me too, I don't know if I can walk home."

"How many beers did you have?"

"I don't know, maybe four or five?"

Soon some of us pair off with boys for the long, cold walk back to our dorm. I remember a guy named Mike who walks me. It's getting late and we needed to make the twelve o'clock curfew. Drunk, we run and giggle arm in arm and only stop to throw snow-balls at each other. At the dormitory door, we share a sweet kiss.

It doesn't feel so cold now.

Back at the dorm, the advice is the same.

"Lie down and put one foot on the floor so you don't get sick."

Too late.

I am already vomiting in the bathroom.

Cortland girls at a later get together

What's The Special?

The job appears in a tiny, one-inch square ad in the New York Times. *Camp counselor wanted at an upscale Catskill Mountain resort.* At eighteen I have finished my freshman year of college, have been a counselor-in-training at a summer camp, and love children. The perfect job for me.

In 1955 there are numerous resorts in the Catskill Mountains, nicknamed the Borsht Belt. This has a vast appeal for hard-working New Yorkers who drive the few hours north to spend a week or two away from the steaming city. They are transported to green mountains where they are greeted with clean air, beautiful forests, and the morning warble of local birds. Most of all you can luxuriate at modern up-to-date hotels with Olympic pools, comfortable lounge chairs, tennis and volleyball courts, elegant night clubs, and best yet, opulent dining rooms.

In these dining halls, there is a wide variety of succulent choices at all three meals. You can order anything or everything you want from the menu. Each night a special is offered. It may be a lovely bouillabaisse, filet mignon, or rack of lamb. The "help" however, never gets more than a whiff.

"Blackman's Hotel," sings the friendly voice. "How can I help you?" Within minutes of stating my meager qualifications, I am offered the job.

"Report to work on July 1st. You are expected to work through August."

The pay is abominable, but I am promised tips each week from the parents. "You will sleep in the barracks, located up the hill near the camp. You will eat in the staff dining room."

After a long bus ride, a taxi drops me at the huge circular driveway of Blackman's Hotel. My terror is coupled with excitement as I drag my suitcases through the sparkling glass doors into the lobby of what seems to be the ultimate in 50's modern design. I am impressed with the long, curved gray and black couches, low round marble coffee tables, touches of red throughout, and abstract paintings on the wall.

I introduce myself to the woman at the front desk who makes a quick call. Immediately there appears another teenaged girl like myself.

"This is Linda, she will show you the ropes."

Linda is a cute curly haired blond with a round face and big smile. I like her immediately. She has worked here before and lives in a nearby town. As we trudge up the hill to the staff barracks she fills me in on the daily routine, the children and the "crazy" parents. We share a small stuffy, wood-paneled room with two cots, two dressers, and an open closet.

The staff dining room is just off the plush, white table-clothed, fine china, main dining room. We can sniff the aroma of luscious roast prime rib, filet mignon, grilled shrimp and desserts flambe. Today the special is lobster florentine. We eat dry hamburgers on stale buns with limp fries. We get Jello or ice cream for dessert.

Waiters and busboys are still working the tables but stop by to say hi to the counselors, swim and tennis instructors, the dance teachers and some office staff. It is a loud and funny group. One busboy stops by to say hello to Linda.

"Introduce me to the new slave laborer." he jokes. He taps me on the shoulder.

"Catch you later to tell you what really goes on here." He is very cute, has a slim, muscular body, with brown eyes and nice curly hair. His name is Turk.

As the evening wanes, I am sleepy, but sit on our porch with others, several of whom are smoking, after a long day. Turk meanders up the hill to the porch and sits down next to me.

"Now little girl, let me tell you what lurks behind this magnificent facade. The wives and children are the guests who spend many weeks at a time here. The husbands come on weekends. It is the wait staff's job to keep these moms happy." A pause. I listen intently.

"That means we compliment them, play tennis with some of the women and dance with some at night. You have probably figured out that tips are the only way you can make any money."

I say, "Ok, how does that work?"

"At the end of each week on Sundays before the men go back to the city, they hand out tips. Keep track of who gives what."

"What if they don't?" I say.

"Well, you might have to ask them to pay up."

"I could never do that."

"Well in the dining room we have our little punishments. Gotta go, see you later."

I later learn that the waiters sometimes spit or urinate in the soup of bad tippers.

The day begins early and we meet our little campers in the kids dining room. We eat cereal, scrambled eggs and toast. The aroma this morning from the main dining room includes hot brewed coffee, baked croissants and breads, danish pastries, omelets, sausages, smoked salmon and french toast.

I have a group of five, all seven years olds, all adorable. One little boy, Davy, quickly becomes my favorite. His blond bowl haircut glistens in the sun. He takes my hand and asks me sweet questions about what we will be doing today. We play games, do arts and crafts, sing songs and go swimming.

At the kids' pool, some of the mothers drop by. I meet Davy's mom, a very cute blond with a straight simple haircut. She is wearing a typical 1950's two-piece bathing suit nicely draped on her slim and shapely body. She needs no makeup on her tanned, radiant skin. Her nails are cut short with a touch of clear nail polish, unlike some of the women who have teased hair, long red nails, and heavy makeup.

"Hi Marion, I'm Jane, Davy's mom. I can see Davy has already taken a liking to you. I'm off to play tennis, see you later."

"So nice meeting you."

On weekends, we don't work as hard. The husbands come from the hot city exhausted and hungry. They love spending time with their wives and children. The kids swim in the big pool with their dads. The meals are particularly sumptuous on the week-ends and the aromas are new. The specials may be ribs, roast beef, the chef's special brisket, or barbeque chicken. Add to that fresh-baked pies, cakes, pastries, and puddings. There is a wide variety of choices at each meal. After dinner, everyone either takes a nice walk down the country road or goes for a late evening swim in the Olympic pool.

As we in the staff dining room are finishing our mac and cheese, we hear the screaming sirens of an ambulance. We all run out to see a heavy-set bald male being lifted out of the pool onto a stretcher. As I look on with dismay, Turk comes up behind me.

"This happens about once a week. These gluttons just eat too much and have heart attacks. That's the kid Davy's father. Gotta go make sure Jane is Ok. See you later."

The later never comes. Davy's dad is brought back to the hotel around midnight. The word gets out that it was just some angina pain.

The mass exodus of men takes place on Sunday afternoon. I am thrilled to receive a twenty-dollar bill from each of four of my camper's parents. I am amazed at the fifty dollars I receive from Davy's dad.

"Thanks so much for taking good care of Davy he really loves you."

"I love him too."

"Keep an eye on my wife Jane for me too, Ok?" I don't know what to say to this and just reply with,

"See you next week, Mr. Green."

The days go by quickly and busily. Linda and I get an occasional day off so we hitchhike to town and to other hotels to meet friends. In the evenings we are allowed to go to the night club to dance and flirt with other staff members when they are not busy "entertaining" the paying guests. I see Turk from time to time and dance with him when he's not busy "taking care" of Jane Green. I am getting to like him more and more but he keeps his distance.

It is mid-August and I am aware that the summer will soon be coming to an end. I am so happy that I took the risk and work here at Blackman's. I have gotten to know all of the staff and so many of the guests and feel comfortable in all the areas of the hotel. I have not, of course, seen any of the beautiful hotel bedrooms and suites occupied by the guests.

One Tuesday afternoon when camp is out, before dinner, I am sitting in a comfortable leather armchair, relaxing in the main lobby. A desk clerk asks me to do a favor.

"Would you mind running up to room 403 to deliver this telegram to Mrs. Green?"

"Not at all."

I take the elevator up. As I am rounding the corner to 403, I stop short. I tiptoe back so as not to be seen. I peek out to see that there in front of room 403, Turk and Jane Green are pressed together against the wall embracing and kissing.

I am horrified and nauseated. I tear down the stairway as fast as I can. Breathless, I tell the desk clerk that no one answered the door and drop the telegram on the desk.

I am outside in the cool late afternoon air trying to breathe.

After several minutes, the desk clerk comes out to tell me that she delivered the telegram herself to Mrs. Green who finally did answer the door.

"It's so sad, this time Mr. Green really did have a heart attack."

Le Car

In June 1960, even more thrilling than my Cortland College graduation was the prospect of getting my driver's license.

I practiced with steady and exciting diligence during my senior year on the streets of Cortland, New York. I felt ready. I knew how to use hand signals—left hand straight out the window for a left turn, bent at the elbow for a right. I could parallel park on either side of the street. I gave it my time and energy.

It was a perfect life moment when the motor vehicle examiner said, "Marion you passed with flying colors."

At age twenty-one, I was ready to return to the big city, the Bronx, New York, my home. To my surprise, my dad had a car waiting for me.

"Marion, this is your graduation present. We hope you like it. Here's to many great experiences driving it."

It was a light blue, bulky, 1955 Chevy convertible. I feigned astonishment and pleasure.

"Dad, Mom, this is great. Thank you so much."

Big hugs and kisses all around. I must admit the Chevy was a bit of a disappointment. Secretly, I had hoped to buy a snazzier car.

On that hot summer day I took Dad for a ride, top-down. The humid breeze mussed my hair and cooled Dad's bald head. It felt so good. We were so exhilarated that we ended up at Jahn's famous ice cream parlor on Fordham Rd. We both enjoyed black and white ice cream sodas and drove home by way of the Bronx Zoo.

I began teaching 5th grade in New Rochelle in the fall and planned to save my money. My boyfriend, Sid, had a red,1959 MG sports car. It was so low down you had to slide into it like a snake. A cool beauty. So much better than my old Chevrolet. But sadly, I could never afford a car like that.

It didn't take long for me to find a magazine ad for the Renault Caravelle. This was the car for me. Built in France between 1958 and 1968, it was small, sleek and smooth. There was plenty of room for two in front and a very small back seat.

66

How could I imagine where the quest for the Caravelle would lead?

By the end of my first year of teaching, I had saved the nearly $2000 I needed to by a brand new, 1961 Caravelle. I remembered my friend, Gary, who I'd met one summer working at Blackman's Hotel. He worked in his father's foreign car dealership in Bridgeport, Connecticut. It was easy to find him. I was happily surprised that he had several Caravelles on the lot and promised to give me a great deal.

"It's so great to hear from you, Marion. I remember all the fun we had at Blackman's. Can you take the train to Bridgeport? I have a few beauties to show you."

"Why not? Sounds great!"

"So, I'll meet you at the station. See you Saturday."

Gary was pretty much as I remembered him. Short and strong, a thick shock of auburn hair and vague acne scars. He must be working out, I thought. He still had the pleasant, broad smile that I remembered.

He was so friendly and gregarious. We hugged and had lots to say.

I was amazed at how quickly I fell in love with the shiny new, red model, just perfect for my size and taste. I had taken lessons on a stick shift at home in preparation for this day. I loved the power and control driving a stick shift gave me. The purchase went smoothly and as promised, the price was right.

As it turned out I would have to stay overnight on Saturday at a motel and drive the car home on Sunday. We decided to have dinner together. As we ate in a nice little Italian restaurant we enjoyed reminiscing over glasses of wine.

It is after midnight when we get to the motel. Gary promises to get me the next day to pick up my new car. He walks me to the motel door.

"Thanks again, Gary. It's been a wonderful day and I love my new car. See you in the morning."

As I open the door I notice he's holding a bottle of Chivas Regal.

"I'm exhausted, I really need to get some sleep."

"Let's just have a nightcap," he says, as he pushes by me into the motel room.

"Really Gary, I don't think so."

"Just one drink, a toast to your new car."

He opens the bottle and pours the liquid into plastic cups. He places the bottle and cups on a little table. The table is complete with two swivel chairs in a corner of the room near the door.

"Just one little drink," he cajoles. He seats himself.

I am so grateful for all of his help that I don't see the harm. We sit on the swivel chairs and drink.

"You are so amazing," he begins. "You know what you want and you go and get it. I love that about you. I'm hoping we can see more of each other."

"I don't know, Gary, you live quite a distance away."

With that he drops to his knees and swings my chair around to face him. Both of his hands are sliding up my thighs under my skirt.

"I really like you a lot, Marion."

I try to get up but his hands move again and are now around my waist, pushing persistently up to my armpits.

"Gary, this is ridiculous. You need to leave."

By now he is leaning over me pressing his lips roughly onto mine. When he speaks again, he is breathless, his voice raspy.

"Just touch me."

Now I am terrified.

My knee automatically thrusts upward into his groan.

He yells out in pain.

"You f..ing bitch, after all I did for you."

"Get the hell out!" I scream. He grabs the bottle and runs out the door.

Shaking with fright I double-lock and bolt the door.

I barely sleep.

I had no way of knowing if he would show up the next day with my car.

Morning came and through the damp breeze from the air conditioner, I could feel the day was warm and sticky.

With reluctance, I spread the motel curtains to peek out. There, sparkling in the sunlight I see Le Car. I gingerly open the door and an envelope falls to the ground.

A note inside reads, "Marion, here are the keys to your new car. I am so sorry about what happened last night. I hope we can meet again. Good luck. Gary."

In a flash, I am out the door and into my sleek new Caravelle. I press my foot on the clutch and ease it into first, then enter the highway. Sliding the gears all the way to fifth I am on the road in my awesome car, headed home.

I never saw Gary again.

Mom

A mother is a daughter's first best friend. The more a daughter knows the details of her mother's life, the stronger the daughter.
— *Anita Diamant*

Bella The Midwife, as told by Ariel

I come from a long line of strong women. But what I find in a junk drawer comes as a complete surprise.

When our family visits our grandparents in New Jersey, my brothers and I love to explore the basement, then go through drawers upstairs for treasures. In one bedroom drawer I find a crumpled box containing stories written by my great grand-mother, Lena-Paula.

Flipping through them I find *Tale of Bella the Midwife.* As I read my granddaughter Ariel's rendering, I realize that Bella is my great, great, great grandmother.

I am fascinated to discover that in 1857 Bella and Jacob are living in a hut in a small town in Poland.

Jacob is a tailor who often travels on a horse-drawn cart to rich landowners to make their clothing. While Bella, clad in rough-hewn, floor-length dresses attends to the childbirths in the village. She uses a cart too, but mostly she walks to see her patients. In winter, the horse-drawn cart is exchanged for a sleigh which she navigates herself. Her layers of bloomers, petticoats, high button shoes, sheepskin jacket, and hat are barely enough to keep out the harsh snow and winds.

On their own tiny plot of land Bella and Jacob grow potatoes, beets, carrots, and turnips. They keep a cow for milk, and chick-ens for eggs, and have an occasional chicken feast.

Bella is trained in the use of herbal medicines, finding them in the fields and forests. She uses them to ease the ailments of her patients.

The story goes that when Bella is old and can no longer walk, she still delivers babies. One day she receives an emergency message from a peasant man whose wife is in desperate need of the midwife. The woman struggles in pain with the baby about to be born. The husband has no time to harness his horse so he carries Bella piggyback to his wife's bedside to deliver the baby.

Years later in 1898, Bella's daughter Sarah (my great, great grandmother), and her husband Hyman hear of the much talked about paradise in America. They leave the village separately. He goes first. They each hitch rides and walk with only their carpet bags of precious items and clothing to Hamburg, Germany. There they board a ship to America.

I would love to meet Bella and ask her how she found the inspiration and courage to do the work she did. I treasure this story of bravery to move my life forward in my quest to follow my dreams.

Ariel

Mom's Story

Sarah has ten pregnancies but only three children live. The first child who lives is a girl named Esther. She dies of Scarlet Fever at age four. Next comes my mother, Lena-Paula.

When Lena-Paula Block is born on December 3, 1900, on the lower east side of New York City, no one knows if the tiny four-pound baby will survive through the year let alone live to age ninety-three. Without incubators, this baby girl is brought home, wrapped in cotton and placed in a men's shoe box near the stove in the kitchen. Luck prevails and Lena-Paula makes it.

Hyman, the philanderer, is seen about town in his snappy clothes and fedora hat.

The household is chaotic. Sarah and Hymie bicker and disagree about everything. Hence their inability to agree on a name for the little baby.

Sarah likes Lena, Hyman wants Paula.

"Paula is more American!" He yells.

"I'm writing Lena on the birth certificate. You can't stop me."

"Well, I'm sick of your complaining and arguing about everything."

"You're sick of me? I'm tired of you running around every night. Don't think I don't know what you do out there. What about us? What about your family?"

"Aach, you don't know what you're talking about!"

The legal name became Lena, but most people called her Paula.

Three years afterward, Abraham is born, and seven years later Mom's sister Fae. Was this an accident? Who knows. Hyman seemed available periodically to impregnate my grandmother. My grandparents stayed together until they reached their seventies when Sarah decided to leave the marriage.

Hyman, it must be said, had some important good qualities. Although his several businesses failed, he was a hard worker. By trade, he was a tailor, but owned a series of grocery stores and finally a women's clothing store.

Lena-Paula becomes a central figure in this fragmented family. She is the brainy one, Abe is the comic, the witty clever one, and Fae is the beauty.

They live in a chaotic household, rife with marital disappointments. Hymie, when not at work, continues to stay out and chase the ladies.

Not surprising that Lena, the oldest, becomes the babysitter and peacemaker.

As time passes the family moves many times owning small, unsuccessful, grocery and women's clothing stores around the city. Both parents work in the stores while the children bring themselves up. They attend many neighborhood schools and learn a lot about life on the streets.

Lena secretly determines to create a life for herself free from family turmoil. The times are ripe for change. Lena in her teens becomes involved in the women's suffrage movement. When she is twenty women finally win the right to vote.

She also has a zest for learning. She fights for her education all the way to Hunter College.

At the end of World War I Lena is in the street celebrating with her friend Ray. On that day she sees the great opera singer Caruso sing from his balcony.

In her twenties, she will see the country struggle with the great depression. She meets her husband, Leo, at a political rally.

They are married in June 1936.

I am born on December 16, 1938.

Hyman, Lena-Paula's father

Sarah, Lena-Paula's mother

The Fresher the Better

On the lower East Side in 1905 grandma Sarah believes that good health is related directly to the food we eat. Above all and at any cost the food has to be fresh.

Fresh now and fresh then are very different. Fresh chicken noodle soup then meant going straight to the poultry market to purchase a live chicken. It meant making the noodles for the soup from scratch.

Grandma chooses the chicken and watches as it is deprived of its life with a sharp scalpel-like instrument, zip, zip, slash. The head rolls back, the blood drips, the wings continue to flap. She carries it home in a sack, every so often feeling a twitch of life. At home, she plucks out all the big feathers. Then she singes off the pin feathers over the wood-burning stove. She salts it and lets it drain in the sink. Later the chicken will be either boiled or roasted.

Grandma's large dining room table is prepared for noodle making by covering it with a huge white, padded sheet. The dough is rolled out with a long narrow rolling pin. It becomes the size of the table. The dough is folded over and over into a roll. With a very sharp knife and magical speed, Grandma cuts very near to her knuckles. She hacks it into very thin noodles. It must be said here that mothers-in-laws judged the worth of the bride-to-be by the swiftness and precision with which she could cut noodles. If you passed the noodle test you were ready for marriage.

When gefilte fish is in order for Passover, a huge live carp is purchased at the fish market. It is dumped from the bucket into the bathtub filled with water where it swims for two days. Grandma Sarah lays the fish on the same long table. This time it's covered with brown butcher paper. She chops the head off with a single blow of a large heavy knife.

As a five-year-old child my mom Lena remembers the fear she felt as she watched the headless fish as it still wriggled.

Sometimes it falls off the table and grandma picks it up, still wiggling, and takes it to the sink to wash it. She then proceeds to fillet it, chop it with onions, adds salt, pepper, matzo flour and eggs. She shapes the mixture into balls, wraps each one in a piece of fish skin and drops them one by one into salted boiling water. This simmers for three hours. When it cools you have delicious gefilte fish in a savory jelly.

Keep in mind that there is no refrigeration. Mom remembers the friendly iceman who delivers a large block of ice every few days. This block is wrapped in a burlap potato sack and slung over his shoulder. He carries it up the long flight of stairs to grandma's apartment. It is placed in the upper portion of the icebox. The ice slowly melts through a tube into a basin on the floor. This basin must be frequently emptied or the kitchen will flood.

The family labors hard every day to provide food for each meal. It begins with shopping every morning at the open vegetable and fruit market, the meat and fish markets, and the grocery. At the grocery, the milk is in a large barrel. The grocer ladles it out into a milk can that the customer brings. Grandma buys flour and yeast for bread and cakes at the same store. Sometimes the sawdust on the floor finds its way into the milk and flour. Cheese and butter are kept on ice and sold by the pound in chunks.

Finally, grandma carries it all home. Many more hours are spent preparing each meal on the wood-burning stove.

Nowadays we can tell it's fresh when we see artificially colored red meat squeezed tight behind see-through plastic. Our milk is very white and homogenized in containers. Our grains must be crispy and sweetened to taste, in the cereal aisle. Our vegetables often come in chip form and moms like to push dehydrated vegetable puffs on their toddlers.

At home, we can't wait to crack open our Cheddar corn Doritos and smell the wonderfully salty, cheesy aroma. We salivate at our first crunchy bite. We love washing it down with a Zero Calorie Coke.

Fresh has to be colorful, crunchy and salty or sweet.
The fresher the better!

The Soap Coupon Doll

Oh Sleep it is a blessed thing
Loved from pole to pole
—The Ancient Mariner, Samuel Coleridge

My grandfather was a sound sleeper. From the minute his head touched the pillow until the ring of the alarm clock in the morning, he slept without moving. The only human being who could wake him was my Grandmother. She would, not so gently, nudge his shoulder to bring him back to reality.

Grandma Sarah saved Kirkman soap coupons. She saved them for two years in order to get my mom a french doll. In 1910 this was the object of longing for this ten-year-old little girl.

When the doll finally arrived Lena-Paula gingerly removed the packaging and found a large, flowered cardboard box. With delicate and trembling fingers she lifted the lid. It was the most beautiful creature she had ever seen. Pink cheeks on porcelain skin, blond curls, delicate features, and blue eyes. The clothes were exquisite, of fine brocade and silk. There were feathers in her plush pink hat. Her dainty feet were shod in fine socks and Mary Jane patent leather slippers. Underneath were a lace-trimmed petticoat and underdrawers. Mom never played with this doll. She placed it safely in its box. It stood upright and open on her bedroom dresser. All she did was look at her and worship.

One Sunday afternoon Mom and Grandma went shopping on bustling 110th Street, in Manhattan. Grandpa Hymie agreed to stay home and take care of Lena's younger brother Abe who was six years old. As you might have guessed, Grandpa immediately fell asleep, his Sunday nap. Abie, a quiet child, played with his books and toys.

Returning two hours later, they could not get into their second-floor apartment because Grandma had forgotten her keys. She rang the bell furiously, banged on the door and shouted, to no avail. Grandpa was asleep.

Finally, they decided to climb up the fire escape. Very cautiously Sarah and Lena made their way up the iron rungs one at a time.

"Oh no! The window is locked," whined Grandma.

"What do we do now?" screeched Lena.

"Hymie, open the window!" she yelled.

They banged and slapped at the window with no result. No use. Where was Abie?

"Abie, Abie, come to the window!" Knocking loudly again. No answer.

In desperation, Grandma Sarah broke a small pane, stuck her hand through and opened the lock. They raised the window and climbed in.

The house was quiet. Hymie was asleep. Brother Abie had disappeared.

What met their gaze when they entered Lena's bedroom was shocking. There, scattered around the room were the tattered remains of the beautiful soap coupon doll. Who else but Abie could have done this? He had done a complete job of dismantling the adored treasure. On the bed they found the clothes, the wig, the hat, the underwear. The ugly cloth body lay twisted with its arms and legs each torn off. The head was decapitated with a big hole on top. The rod lying beside it had been used to thrust the wig and hat into place.

Lena screamed so loudly the whole neighborhood must have heard.

Grandma was yelling, cursing and crying.

"That God-damned kid, where is he? I'm going to kill him. Abieeeee!"

"Where are you?"

They searched the house and finally found him hiding under his bed, in the farthest corner, almost unreachable. Grandma pulled Abe out and gave him the worst spanking of his young life, smacking his head, arms, and butt.

As Abe howled at the top of his lungs, Grandma yelled uncontrollably and Mom screamed pitifully, while Grandpa slept.

It was only when Grandma gave Grandpa a not so gentle nudge that he finally woke up.

The Featherbed

My Grandma Sarah arrived in NYC in 1898. She brought her two most precious possessions: her three-year-old daughter, Esther, and her goose down featherbed. Tiny Esther posed no problem since she could walk. But the elephantine featherbed had to be carried, lugged, pulled and watched over for fear it might be stolen.

My grandfather met my grandma at Ellis Island.

"Oh Sarah, you finally made it. I am so happy to see you and oh, look at little Esther, so beautiful! She was just a baby when I left."

As they hugged, grandpa looked over grandma's shoulder, noticing the huge bundle.

"Sarah, what is that?"

"Oh, that's my goose down featherbed," she said with pride.

"Throw it in the ocean," came his derisive and angry reply. "This is not Poland, this is America."

Grandma did not heed his demand and schlepped the featherbed with her to their furnished, three-room apartment that grandpa had rented. It was a cold-water railroad flat complete with the odors and noises of their strange immigrant neighbors. The walls were so thin they could hear the screaming fights of families around them. Not least was their own bickering which always escalated into full-blown rows. This added to the cacophony.

"This is where you bring me and Esther? Where is the peace and quiet?"

Even though the walk-up was on the third floor, it could not blot out the howling, endless congestion on the streets.

"I'm doing the best I can. You are always crying and angry. I'm sick of it."

But grandpa had to admit that during the cold winter nights on the lower east side the featherbed was a great comfort.

Unfortunately, to everyone's regret, and grandma's lifelong sorrow, little Esther died of Scarlet Fever at the age of four. The featherbed remained.

My mother, Lena-Paula was born shortly after, to be followed by her brother Abe and sister Fae. The family moved to Brooklyn, to a steam-heated apartment. The featherbed came along.

At age ten, Lena was a thin, wiry young girl. Grandma thought it was time she helped with the housework. On days off from school, among other chores, she was assigned to clean her parent's bedroom.

Their bed was chin high on Lena, the pillows enormous. There on top was the featherbed. She could never get the monster to lie evenly. If you flattened it on one side, it would puff out on the other. If both sides were straightened, it would puff in the middle. She would climb onto the bed to smooth it with no luck. It had a life of its own.

"Mom, come in here to help me. I can't do this by myself."

"I know, I know. I'm coming."

They would tame the wild beast together, finally smoothing a heavy bedspread on top of it.

When Lena was sixteen grandma Sarah discovered a merchant who made comforters out of featherbeds. He removed all the feathers and was able to carefully stuff them again into two colorful patterned comforters. Elaborate stitching held the feathers in place. No more lumps.

The younger sister, Fae, got married first. Grandma gave her one of the comforters. But Fae's husband preferred an electric blanket. Fae gave the comforter to a home for the aged.

Grandma Sarah kept the other comforter at home. When she died in 1953, Lena found the worn and faded comforter among the many odd and useless possessions.

Lena gave it to a charity organization with little hope that it would ever be used again.

Lena-Paula

Lena and sister Fae

Early on my mother loved school and became a straight-A student. To her dismay, while she'd rather have been reading and studying, she was assigned to take care of baby Fae every day after school while Sarah worked in the store.

She loved her little sister but resented the diaper changes, having to boil them later in a big pot on the stove. She worried about the child's asthma attacks. She had to sit with her in a steamy bathroom or take her outside on cold winter nights. Most of all she was troubled by the little girl's temper tantrums.

One day, in the spring of 1913 the family is living on 110th street. Lena-Paula, of course, has to babysit. She is 13, Abe is 10 and Fae only 3. They live on the top of a very steep hill. The children sit on the stoop of their brownstone house. Abe and Lena are playing jacks and Fae is in her stroller.

Suddenly, a group of boys appears.

"Abie, where's the money you owe us?"

"I don't owe you anything, stupid."

"You lost the bet, so pay up."

"Not on your life, loser."

As the boys begin to tussle, Abe yells,

"Hold my glasses, Lena."

Lena runs into the fray to grab the glasses.

She doesn't see the stroller start its slow roll down the hill. When she realizes what is happening all she can do is look with horror as it picks up speed. Running after it screaming, Lena watches the stroller land upside down in the street. The crash brings traffic to a halt. A small crowd gathers.

When Lena rights the stroller she finds baby Fae lying still, ashen and silent. A big bump has formed on the child's forehead. Lena is crying uncontrollably.

"Oh God, what have I done?"

She picks up the little tot and kisses her face, again and again. She frantically rubs her back. Finally, there is a flicker in the baby's eyes and weak whimpering.

After that day, Lena secretly determines to create a life for herself free from family turmoil.

For most of their lives, Lena-Paula would be the mediator, the voice of reason, the problem solver. Abe escaped family turmoil with humor, hanging out with friends and winning dance contests. Boys discovered the beautiful, auburn-haired, violet-eyed Fae, who stayed away from home as much as possible.

As a teenager, Lena-Paula becomes involved in the women's suffrage movement. Freedom is still a dream because of her strong family attachment. She has a special empathy for her long-suffering mother. For the rest of their lives, Lena-Paula would be the mediator, the voice of reason, the problem solver.

When it came time for college, money was scraped up for the boy to go. Abe attended Podiatry School. Lena-Paula went to secretarial school. It was only later that she completed her college degree on her own.

When she is 20 women finally win the right to vote, but girls are still far from free to pursue their dreams or talents. The most important female duty is to find a suitable husband.

Lena had a small frame and a sweet face. She was a good athlete and a speedy runner. She, like Abe, was nearsighted.

She wore round wire-rimmed glasses. The refrain went, "Boys don't make passes at girls who wear glasses." She didn't care. She wore no makeup and had flyaway hair. She wore less than attractive clothes. Lena was an intellectual and feminist.

Fae, on the other hand, always brushed her long auburn hair until it glistened, wore makeup and spent every cent on beautiful clothing. At this time Hyman owned a women's clothing store and Fae would spend Saturdays modeling the suits, dresses, and coats for customers. She was a great dancer and went to dances with her brother. There she met eligible young men many of whom fell in love with her.

As the oldest daughter, Lena-Paula was expected to marry first. This was not to be. Quite the opposite. Fae, with her great beauty and poise, met Albert, a lawyer. Hyman was thrilled. But Sarah mourned the fact that my mother had not yet found a husband. Fae's wedding, therefore, was a terribly sad event for her.

Next, Abe found a young woman, Laura, who was a teacher. This was meant to be a happy event but there was no pleasure in it for Sarah.

She cried for days before and after each wedding.

Lena-Paula was not sad for herself. She had a great secretarial job, loved her friends, and went to night school at Hunter College. Finally, in her late 30's, Mom met her sweet and funny husband Leo.

I am so lucky they did.

A Woman Must, 1934

Lena-Paula

(As Lena-Paula grows older, Mother Sarah shares her concern)
Daughter you are not married

You are thirty-four and not married

Mother, I have a life, I love this life
Why, Mother do you harp?
Why must you cry?

I cry for you daughter because you must
A woman must
A woman must marry to be safe
I can't stop crying

Momma you cry too much
Because I am the oldest
Is that why?
You cry about your own marriage
Cry Cry Cry

Daughter your brother Abe
He is married
Your baby sister Fae
She is married
I cried at their weddings for you
Cry Cry Cry

Momma, I am at Hunter College
I have a job
I have friends
I fight for women's rights
I am happy, momma

My daughter, I love you so much
Fix your hair
Throw out the glasses
Wear tighter clothes, show your figure

Momma, I have a lover

Daughter, will he marry you?

My Mom, 1990

(Lena has grown old)

She sits alone on the screened-in porch
Looking at the lilac bush
Its fragrance brings memories of first love
She closes her eyes
She is 90

Mom is tiny and a bit bent now
Her wrinkles tell a story
Bright hazel eyes still gleam with specks of brown
and green in the sunlight
She is 90

She waits for me to come
Can we walk today Marion?
On the shady path?
I can no longer walk alone
I am 90

We stroll along slowly, the weather is mild
Walking arm in arm, we prop each other up
We are strong together
Marion I cannot care for myself anymore
What should I do?
I am 90

Lena, Give me Your Teeth

Mom and Dad are hard workers. They love living in New York City. When I am born, we became an inseparable threesome. We do everything together, enjoying the fun of city life.

Time passes without much notice. I marry and have children of my own. We live in new cities, Washington and Boston, finally ending up in New Jersey. Mom and Dad move to New Jersey to be nearer to us.

After Dad dies on July 4th,1984, Mom lives alone in her little attached house for seven years. By then she is ninety-one years old. Mom has become tiny and frail. I remember the day she sat me down and said, "Marion, I can't take care of myself anymore. Can you find me a place to live?"

Finding Greenwood House, in Ewing Township near Trenton, is easy. I hear many stories about what a wonderful home it is. The transition from the privacy of your own home to a nursing home is a true test of strength. As Mom always said, "Old age is not for sissies." But true to her nature she soon grows to love her time there.

What strikes you first, when you enter the lobby of Greenwood House, is its spacious beauty. Next, there is a lovely food aroma, not the expected nasty old age bodily smells. When you look further, your eyes scan a sea of wheelchairs with shriveled, bent over people. Most often their mouths are open. Are they alive?

"Oh my God, is this where I'm going to put my Mom?" I later realize that when awake, these people are interesting, alert and funny.

The social worker is explaining that everyone gets a wheelchair to push for help with walking and for rides. Mom breezes through the interview with amazing grace.

"I do have to tell you," says the social worker, "We don't have a separate Alzheimers wing. Those residents have separate rooms but are free to roam around."

We sign the papers.

Mom enjoys the entertainment, the food, the discussion group, and ceramics. Everyone is very kind. She particularly loves bath time.

"Marion you won't believe this," she laughs, "They strap you onto a seat and immerse you in bubbling warm water. They soap you up and rinse you off. Then they gently dry you. It's lovely. The towels are so soft."

One night of a full moon, several Alzheimer's patients are struggling. There is a lot of screaming and moaning. Mom is confused by the commotion. Many of these residents are disoriented and begin to wander through the halls. Suddenly one woman climbs into bed with her. There is much screaming and shouting. Mom yells for help.

It takes a couple of hours to calm and medicate several wanderers.

At three a.m. all is quiet. The nurses begin to make their rounds. Mom is finally asleep. A nurse taps her on the shoulder.

"Lena, Lena, wake up dear. Give me your teeth."

Mom is shaken and says, "What?"

"Lena, give me your teeth."

"I can't give you my teeth." The nurse is getting annoyed.

"Lena, give me your teeth!"

"How can I give you my teeth, these are MY teeth. Not false!"

"I am so sorry."

Dad

A father holds his daughter's hand for a short while, but her heart forever. - *Unknown*

My Dad, Leopold, pictured as a child, on the right

Old Men In Baseball Hats

There is something about old guys in baseball hats, especially if they wear the right jeans, work shirts, and good dockers, that I find appealing. I am sure it has something to do with my age and adaptation to the realities of life and death.

I certainly am aware of the fact that beneath the cap one is bound to encounter balding, thinning, comb-overs and buzz cuts on the few hairs that are left. But the baseball cap seems to make it seem okay.

The earliest baseball caps were worn by the Brooklyn Dodgers in 1900. They were soft pliable cotton. During the 1940s, latex rubber became the stiffening material inside the hat and the modern baseball cap, with logo, was born. They were only worn by the players. Old photographs of fans attending games look like a sea of dark Fedora hats, under which sat men in wool suits, stiff collars, and ties. No women. My father, an avid baseball fan, was among them.

My Dad, Leopold, or Leo, was the youngest of four children. He had two brothers, Henrich (Henry), Maximilian (Max), and sister Urellia. They were born in Austria around the turn of the century. Until tragedy struck they were a stable upper-middle-class family. Their father, Bernard, was in the business of importing and exporting chocolate, nuts, dry fruit and candy. Dad's mother Marie was the proper mother and homemaker. Unfortunately, in 1910 Bernard died suddenly in his forties, leaving the family helpless. Their best alternative was to move to the United States.

Leo, age 7, arrived with his mother in 1914. The siblings had arrived earlier and all moved west. Dad alone, with his mom, struggled to make it in New York City. It didn't take long, however, for him to discover baseball and the Yankees.

When Marie died, Dad was twenty years old. He went to live alone at the YMCA on 21st St. He was free now, after work, to have fun and go to as many Yankee games as he pleased. He enjoyed arriving at games early to watch practice and get autographs. The Yankees made him feel pride for his home team and for being a part of the incredible New York experience.

By then Dad had begun to lose his hair. He experienced early pattern baldness inherited from his father. To compensate he became an immaculate dresser. He wore perfectly starched shirts, always dry-cleaned suits, fine silk ties and of the required fedora hat. Dressing well helped his confidence as he began his career as a respected salesman.

Dad met my mother in 1936, married in 1937 and they had me in 1938. His only child, I brought joy and laughter into his life. We became an inseparable threesome. We loved all the amazing opportunities available to us in the city. Dad used his Argus camera to capture, in black and white, photos inside museums and restaurants, and outside in parks, zoos and on the streets, of his little family. He and Mom always dressed up, he in his felt fedora, in winter, and a straw Panama hat in summer. Mom, too, wore a variety of hats, often with little veils.

As years passed, styles became more and more casual. Dad, still a perfectionist, always kept up with fashion. He began to joke about his baldness, which was now complete, except for the bottom fringe.

"Hair today, gone tomorrow," he always said and would toss his head back while pretending to run his fingers through what used to be hair. Now he cultivated a neatly trimmed mustache and began to wear a variety of hats. He stuck to the summer Panama but added golf hats and a straw boater. He loved his newsboy hat and even had a pork pie hat.

Dad died in 1984 before the baseball cap became the rage.

But I remember buying him a Yankee's cap which he loved to wear around the house and neighborhood.

He looked very cool.

I think we have lost a lot by wearing ultracasual clothing for all we do. On the other hand, it is so easy to travel and go to restaurants and theaters in comfortable clothing and shoes. I love that women, as well, wear baseball hats for any reason that strikes them—to block the sun, on a bad hair day, or just to complete an outfit. The children and grandchildren have followed suit.

Who knows what will come next.

My Name is Leopold, The Letter

Dear Marion,

By the time you find this, I will already have passed on. As you can see I left this account of my life in the top drawer of your desk under all the papers. I am certain you will get to it eventually.

You know me well enough to know that I am always reticent and apprehensive about sharing too many personal feelings and stories about my life. But now I want you to know at least as much as I can remember.

I was born in Chernovitz, Austria, on February 21, 1907. I was the youngest of four children born to Marie and Bernard Sternberg. My siblings were all a good deal older than I. Heinrich was the oldest, next came Maximilian, then Aurelia, the only girl. I, the baby, was named Leopold.

We were fortunate to be living in the Austrian-Hungarian region of Europe ruled by the benevolent emperor, Franz Joseph. He was known for his humanitarian concept of government, unusual in that part of the world. Germany was ruled by the Kaiser, Russia by the Czar.

We were unfortunate, on the other hand, that my father died in 1908 when I was only an infant. He had risen in position to the level of a respected wholesale businessman. He imported coffee, tea, sugar, cocoa, chocolates, assorted candies, dry fruits, and nuts. Four of his salesmen traveled throughout the Austrian-Hungarian empire. They sold to hotels, confectionary stores, and bakeries. The merchandise was imported from Germany, Switzerland, Italy, and Turkey. We were considered members of the bourgeois class.

As members of the bourgeois class, we lived in a well-appointed townhouse, had servants, and I, as a baby, was nursed by a peasant woman because the lady of the house, my mother, found feeding babies this way distasteful. I actually do remember the big woman, with many children, who fed me.

The death of my father, as you can imagine, lead to the complete destruction of my family. We ultimately had to leave Europe for America. We did, however, escape the Holocaust during which all our remaining relatives were murdered by the Nazi's.

My brother Heinrich, who was already twenty years old, was in the Austrian army, far removed from our lives, so he was no help. The business was left in the hands of my mother and brother Max who was eighteen, neither having any experience. Sister Rella was only fifteen. After a few years of struggle, and one comedy of errors after another, they finally had to claim bankruptcy. The bankruptcy laws were so strict that we had to choose between jail and leaving the country. A letter was sent to uncle Max in New York City explaining the urgency of our need to leave Austria at once.

Marion, you can only imagine the reluctance, trepidation, and fear that my mother experienced knowing she would have to leave her home, her relatives and dear friends. Brother Maximilian stayed on to continue the clean up of the business. Sister Rella had chosen to stay behind as well. What awaited was the unknown. Because we were only allowed suitcases on board the S.S. Scharnhorst, which would leave from Hamburg Germany, we had to sell everything else.

On a cold wintry January morning, in 1913, before my seventh birthday, a horse and carriage came to carry mother and me to the train station in Vienna. We were about to embark on the first leg of the journey. Mother dressed in her complete Victorian-era outfit; a long, nearly floor-length velvet skirt, and a high, lacy necked, thick cotton blouse. Beneath she always wore her petticoats and pantaloons. I must mention, too, the torturous laced corset, which often caused shortness of breath. I wore top to bottom long underwear beneath my rather scratchy gray suit. A young boy always donned nickers and boots. Mother and I would never be seen outside of the house without our hats. We made an elegant pair.

We had to wait in the train station overnight, sleeping on benches. When we discovered that our train, first to Berlin, would not leave for another 24 hours, we checked into a small hotel near the train station. We had a nice room with a bath. Exhausted as we were, Mother began to scrub the already spotless sink and bathtub. I fell asleep immediately. The next morning Mother proceeded to wash and scrub me in the same, true Viennese-German fashion. We had breakfast in the hotel restaurant.

Our train to Berlin was halted at the German border where customs officials asked to see our passports. They examined our baggage very carefully and methodically, again in true German fashion. It seemed forever. Throughout the journey, there was always the sense that they would find something wrong. Although we had nothing to hide, we were asked endless questions and finally our passports were stamped, "In Order."

Another long tedious ten-hour ride before we arrived in Berlin. Again we had to find a hotel to get some sleep, a meal, and a hot tub. It would be two weeks before we could leave for Hamburg. This hotel was on a quiet side street. It was old but immaculately clean. With no elevator, Mother and I had to drag our suitcases up three flights of stairs.

For me the most fun was always eating our meals in restaurants where the food was hot and delicious. We ate succulent wursts, weiner schnitzel and spaetzle dumplings. For dessert we often had apple strudel. Mother made sure that I sat up straight, that my napkin was carefully placed on my lap and that I ate precisely, with a knife and fork. She taught me to pull out her chair first and help her to push it in, just like a little man. Here I was just turning seven with a man's responsibility. This burden would grow progressively worse with time.

My recollection of Berlin is rather vague. I do remember that it snowed most of the time and like all big cities it was bustling. We noticed more than the usual number of military personnel in the streets. This was an ominous sign, for in fact, World War I broke out the summer of that year.

The train trip to Hamburg which took fourteen hours, seemed endless as there were many stops along the way. Another two-week stay at yet another hotel in Hamburg seemed to pass quickly. There we were, on a clear Saturday morning, in a rickety motor cab on our way to the pier. We arrived to find a long line of people waiting to board.

The inspectors seemed quite efficient because it wasn't long before they were again examining our papers, passports, and luggage. Everything "In Order." We were given a deck cabin with a double-decker bed and cot, even a mini bathroom. The S.S. Scharnhorst was a small steamer that had seen better days.

As luck would have it, we encountered several sea squalls along the way. My mother later would retell this stormy voyage over and over again. Needless to say, my mother and I, along with all the other passengers were always seasick and were confined to our cabin for several days. After surviving the cruel Atlantic for two weeks, we were able to eat dinner in the dining room. Suddenly, another storm was upon us, causing the boat to sway with extreme intensity. My chair toppled over and I fell on my head, causing a nasty, bloody gash. I was rushed to the infirmary where the doctor stitched the wound. My head was bandaged, which later would cause a big problem with the admitting doctor on Ellis Island.

The day before we landed word had gotten around that we were to enter New York harbor in the morning. This, of course, created great excitement among the passengers. I doubt that anyone slept that night. The next morning, after breakfast, all the passengers gathered on the deck. The tension mounted when suddenly a few tug boats appeared. They were to lead the way. The S.S. Scharnhorst was slowly tugged toward Ellis Island. The Manhattan skyline and the Statue of Liberty were now visible. We were all overcome with joyous emotion. Everyone was crying, laughing and slapping each other on the back. It all seemed so unreal.

Miraculously we were about to land in the new world, "The Promised Land."

Little did we know that our troubles were just about to begin.

My Name is Leopold, This is America?

Dearest Marion,

By now you are assuming that mother and I have arrived safely in America and that life is beautiful. No such luck. It is still 1913, I am 7 years old. Here is what happened on Ellis Island.

It is early morning on a sunny day, when Mother and I walk down the gangplank in a line with scores of other immigrants, as we are now called, dragging our overstuffed leather suitcases. We are met by a group of customs officials who check our passports and luggage. Like sheep, we are taken to a vast auditorium with narrow floor to ceiling windows. We sit on benches with hundreds of people waiting for the physical examination.
"Mama, I have to go the bathroom."
Mama and I, only able to speak German, wave to a nurse attendant with a white coat, a harsh face and a hair bun.
"Schprechen Sie Deutch?" Mama says. Miraculously she did.
This thin, matronly woman leads me down a dark hallway to a large, prison-like bathroom, with rows of urinals and toilets. Several men are urinating, a frightening sight. She promises to wait for me outside. I find a closed booth. To my surprise she does wait. I am so grateful.
We become aware that the physical exam is the most terrifying of all. Many people are turned away and sent back because of Tuberculosis and other infectious diseases. After hours of waiting, having eaten only crackers and milk, suddenly we hear a shrill voice and stomping boots. A customs clerk in uniform comes clumping down our aisle, yelling, "Sternberg, Sternberg!"
He escorts us into a cubicle, divided by a white screen, where a doctor with a long white coat is seated. He is young, angular and mustached with wire-rimmed glasses.
His first words in German are, "Was ist das auf dein kopf?" What is this on your head? My head is still swathed in bandages, which we should have removed, from my fall on the ship. He proceeds to remove the bandages and angrily complains, "This is infected." He stands up and leaves the cubicle.

Every minute is now an eternity. Will we be detained? Will we be sent back? Mother, always too sensitive, too emotional, starts to cry and moan.

"Mein kind, Mein kind!" "My child!"

The doctor finally returns with an older more experienced physician. Mother, now, is blubbering about how I had fallen in the dining room, on the ship, during the terrible storm at sea. This doctor takes a quick look at my injury, pulls a long swab stick from a jar, dips it into a brown solution and roughly applies it to the wound. My painful screaming and yelling, I'm sure, can be heard and echoed throughout the facility. If one were superstitious, you might say that this was a portent of things to come.

Surprisingly, from then on, the examination goes rather smoothly. It seems they are basically looking for infectious diseases and neither Leopold nor Marie Sternberg have any. We are healthy. They examine our eyes, ears, noses, throat, heart, and lungs. They ask us too many questions. The doctor finally hands us a paper saying that we have passed the physical.

We are directed to a room marked HIAS, Hebrew Immigration Aid Society.

My Name is Leopold, The Apartment

Dear Marion,

Here we are again in a holding pen on Ellis Island. This is where thousands of immigrants, each with hopes and dreams, converge. Mother and I find ourselves assigned by ethnic background to a smaller room holding about 50. We sit in rows waiting for our name to be called.

"Mama, I am so tired. How long must we wait to go to our apartment in New York City?"

"Darling, I don't know. Here rest your head on my lap."

I must have dozed for some time because I am jerked out of sleep with a loud, "Sternberg!"

We are taken to a desk where we meet the social worker Mrs. Rosenzweig. She has a sweet smile and curly brown hair.

Now she speaks Yiddish, which Mama understands.

To me, she says, "Do bist a shana boychick."

"You are a pretty boy."

"Danka schoen," Mama replies.

Mrs. Rosenzweig tells us that Uncle Max is waiting for us at our new apartment at 399 East 13th Street.

"You will take the ferry to Manhattan. Here, I am pinning these nice big tags on your coats for identification."

She hugs us as we leave for the ferry.

From the ferry, we have a final look at the Statue of Liberty. As we approach our new city, I feel a thrill.

A small bus is being cranked up as we arrive. It has been sent by HIAS, Hebrew Immigrant Aid Society. The chubby driver helps us with the valises.

"You don't have much to schlepp," he notes, in Yiddish. Mother begins to cry.

"We are left with nothing. Why me?" she weeps.

"Don't worry, I am taking you to meet your Uncle Max. He is a nice man, the neighborhood butcher."

As we bump along on cobblestone streets I see the beautiful Hudson River.

The bus is turning suddenly and we are under an elevated train. As the light fades, as if in a tunnel, we are struck by the flotsam and jetsam of humanity. Strange odors of food, garbage, and animal waste are assault my nostrils. Derelicts are sprawled on the sidewalks. It is the Bowery. Mama is pressing a lace hand-kerchief to her nose.

We come into the light again as the bus is jerking to a halt on the lower east side, at 399 East 13th Street. Uncle Max is waiting.

Uncle Max is my mother's older brother who has found his way to New York and is working as a butcher for a large packing company. He is tall, with a neatly groomed mustache, wearing a tweed suit and bowler hat. He is making his best impression.

"Oh, shvesta," (sister) "It is so good to see you and your "shana zun".

"Vos is der nomen, Boychick?"

"My name is Leopold." I proudly say in English. I learned to say this on Ellis Island.

"Well then, well said. Now that you are in America your name will be Leo." Uncle Max is smiling and shaking my hand.

" And how old are you boychick?"

"I am eight years old, uncle." Again in English.

"Let me show you your apartment. Now don't get your hopes up, it is not what you are used to vet's, Marie. In Austria, I remem-ber the fine house you had, the many beautiful furnished rooms, the bathrooms with hot water and the splendid kitchen. Here you will have none of that. You must be strong. You will get used to it."

399 is an old, neglected, railroad tenement house. We walk up a stoop of too many steps. We are first jarred by the horrible stench of cabbage, stewed meat, sweat, whiskey, and human fe-ces. This gas lit shambles houses twenty families. Our apartment is on the fourth floor so we are again dragging our pathetic leather suitcases up the stairs.

We are right under the elevated tracks so we can hear trains roaring by.

Sharing the two toilets per floor with three other families will come to be a challenge. There is always much screaming and banging on doors.

"Are you done yet?"

"What the hell are you doing in there?"

"Get out, I have an emergency!"

In a railroad flat the rooms follow each other in a straight line. As we enter the mid-sized kitchen with a crude wooden floor, we see in front of us a large tub where Mother will do all the dishes and clothes washing. This is where she will give me my Friday night bath. There is no hot water. So water will have to be boiled on the gas stove.

The other rooms are considered furnished. Two bedrooms with old beds that have stained mattresses assault our eyes. The living room with ancient, decaying furniture insults our sensibilities. Mother is crying.

Uncle Max tries to be encouraging.

"I will help you get this place into shape. There are several social work agencies in the city that can help too."

One way Uncle Max helps us is to introduce us to the 12th Street Bath House. It is between 2nd and 3rd Avenues. It is utilized by all the people in the neighborhood without bathtubs. There are separate sections for men and women. Mother and uncle Max make it a habit to go at least once a week to the baths, where there are clean towels and steam rooms. I am too young to go.

A few months go by and uncle Max is turning out to be a crude and inconsiderate man. He lives alone down the street but takes advantage of my mother's hospitality. She is feeding him three meals a day and washing his dirty underwear.

"Sister, get me a glass of shnapps."

"Marie, cook me your best noodle pudding."

And to me, "Boychick, pull off my boots."

"Boychick, go down the street for a newspaper."

We are praying that uncle Max finds a wife.

Mother toils and scrubs away endlessly, never getting the apartment really clean to her satisfaction.

Uncle Max

My Name is Leopold, Where is the Light?

Dearest Marion,

As my struggles continue in America, my oldest brother, Heinrich (Henry) and my sister Urella remain in Austria. Middle brother Max has already come to the U.S. leaving the decaying family business to his brother and sister. These are the war years, 1914-1918. World War I is raging. Heinrich has completed his time in the Austrian Army. He and my sister work on what was left of the family business and eventually have to claim bankruptcy.

After the war, in 1919, my sister is 25 years old. According to Victorian culture she should have been married by now. Her prospects, in truth, are limited. Although she has beautiful skin and a nice figure, her features are irregular and her personality dower. Smiling comes with great difficulty.

In Austria, my mother Marie has put away the family jewels. They are held, for safekeeping with a trusted banker. They consist of cut diamonds, rubies, and several emeralds, along with gold jewelry carefully inlaid with gems. This dowry attracts Willy Mann who pursues Urella and marries her within the year. He has aspirations.

They arrive in the states in the early 20's and settle in Louisville, Kentucky where he opens a dry goods store. This will eventually become a big success. They have a son who they name Bernard, named after my father.

Marion, I have to tell you that this was not a good marriage. They are not compatible in many ways.

"Rella, Why do you dote on our son so much?"
"Because YOU pay no attention to me! Bernie loves me!"
"If your housekeeping was better I might pay attention to you more."
"All you do is work day and night."
"Someone has to work to keep this family going."
"Don't you love me anymore?"
"If you stopped eating bonbons and lost some weight, I might."

Brother Max, who is now living with us in New York, resents the fact that my mother has turned over the family jewels to my sister. He claims that he has to bear the brunt of our misfortune, therefore he has a legitimate claim to a fair share of the jewels.

"After all I do for you. I at least have a good job, (working for a hat manufacturer). I bring in good money and help pay the bills. I translate English for you."

"It was you, (mother says through clenched teeth) Max, and your inept handling of the business that ruined us. Then you go running away to leave it all to Henrich and Rella to figure out. You deserve nothing."

Marion, this acrimony persisted until she died.

Marion, it will not surprise you to learn that brother Max was always plotting and planning his escape from his ties with me and mother.

In 1923 I am 16 years old. We have moved from 399 13th St. To 3rd St. and 1st Ave. It is an improvement. It is on the 2nd floor with an actual bathroom with a toilet and bathtub. We have acquired some meager furniture and Mother sets to work cleaning, scrubbing, and disinfecting every inch.

Mother still maintains what is left of the linens, dishes, and silverware which were sent to us after the war. She spends hours lovingly washing and ironing the linens, polishing the silver and placing napkins between the dishes. She dreams of her lost life in Europe.

"Look, Leo, at these beautiful things. Do you remember how we used to live in Austria?"

"Yes, Momma, I do remember, but we are here now. We have to make the best of it."

"There is no best here, boychik, nothing will ever be the same for me. Maybe for you it will be better."

Suddenly Max is married to a hat designer, ten years his senior. He has moved to the Grand Concourse. Very ritzy.

Millenary in NYC is big business. The word millenary is derived from the word Millenar, because Milan, Italy, in the 1920s and 30s is the capital of hat design. Everyone in the U.S. and in Europe wears hats every day. Both men and women will never be seen outside of their houses without a hat. The industry grows to include ribbons, laces, feathers, and veiling. That, Marion, is how I ultimately got involved in the millenary business in NY.

Much to Max's regret, his wife contracts cancer and dies within a year, leaving nothing.

"Why me?"

He rails, "What have I done to deserve this?"

Despondent and grief-stricken Max picks up and leaves for California.

I am barely 18 and now have complete responsibility for the support of myself and Mother.

My Name is Leopold, Survival

Dearest Marion,

How I managed to grow up, find meaningful work, get married and have you is beyond my comprehension. I suppose the actual fight for survival made me stronger.

Ever since I can remember I always found a way to work and read. Work and read, work and read. After school, to avoid going home, I often did my homework in the public library on 14th street, near 2nd Ave.

Even as a small child I have always loved to listen. I love to hear Mother humming old tunes. I love the clatter of her pots and pans as she makes chicken soup, kasha and bow ties, and noodle kugel. I am accustomed to every creak and rattle in our apartment.

My ears are attuned to the threats of the streets. I learn quickly to trust my fears and avoid the sounds of danger. I am learning, too, that there is an intelligent and educated world beyond my small one. I am fascinated by the daily speeches in Union Square Park. I hear street corner orators enthusiastically spewing forth about women's rights, Christian Science, Socialism, Anarchism, Capitalism, Vegetarianism and Atheism. I am ten years old. The year is 1917.

In the beginning, by age 8, I am making deliveries. I am lucky to find a friend in the apartment next to ours. His name is Jakob. We are partners in work and play, and crime, in making deliveries, escaping beatings by street gangs and avoiding the police. We will deliver anything for anyone. We are like the rodents in the stifling alleyways, scurrying and slipping either toward or away from seamy destinations.

As I mentioned before, we are living on the crowded Lower East Side among poor, struggling immigrants. Here, in the bowels of the city I learn about life. I learn about gambling, alcoholism, prostitution, homosexuality, and crime.

We start with newspaper deliveries, move on to package deliveries and deliveries of money. Jakob and I acquire two old rickety bicycles with baskets in front, giving us newfound speed and freedom.

One morning, as I walk along the street, I see sitting on a stoop a heavily made-up woman, in scanty dress and fishnet stockings.

She yells, "Hey Leo, it's me Greta. Come here, give me a kiss darlin' I miss you honey."

I am too young to purchase her wares, but I like her perfume and the candy and money she gives me for deliveries.

"I need you to take this package to Louie, the pawnbroker, on 14th street."

She hands me a small package wrapped in brown paper and string.

"He will give you money in an envelop, Leo. Do not open that envelop."

"Ok, Greta," I say.

"Now come here and give me a kiss."

I like her fragrant, moist kisses and get a sweaty hug as well.

Later in the day Jakob and I are pulled into a hallway by Mrs. Lubin.

"Boys, I need you to get me a bottle of gin from the bar. The damn bartender won't allow me in. Here's fifty cents and pennies for you. Do not tell my husband. He wants to kill me. Go, now, quick."

Delivery of money from and to the bookmakers can be dangerous.

"Listen, little boy, if you steal even one cent I will know it. I will cut your tongue out and shove it down your throat."

At the end of the day, we have earned some spending money. I bring it home to Mom who doesn't ask.

Before my brother Max abandons us for California, he helps us move to the Bronx. I am 16 years old. Our apartment is located at 2718 Morris Ave. This apartment is quite nice, two bedrooms, kitchen, living room, and bathroom in a quiet neighborhood. My brother is paying the rent of $37.00 per month.

Max gets me a job at a company, A&H Veith. It is located at 5th Avenue at 37th Street. They are importers of millenary, dress trimmings and fabrics. I make myself generally useful. I run errands, fill orders and wait on customers. My starting salary is $12.00 per week. Through a succession of raises, my salary is upped to $20.00 per week.

For another year Max helps to supplement our income, but one summer day, with little to say, he departs for California.

Mother cries bitter and angry tears. She violently throws out every single meager possession that Max leaves behind. She scrubs away the remains of his odor and his presence in every room.

The year is 1925, I am 18 years old. My salary is inadequate to meet our daily needs. I decide, at work, to approach my sales manager, George Brooks. I politely make known to him my dire home situation. I tell him that I would like to become a salesman.

With a kind voice, "I will discuss this matter with Mr. Adolph Veith." He is president of the firm.

Within a few weeks my career as a salesman is launched. In a short time I am averaging about $35.00 per week, which is sufficient to support mother and myself.

Mother is crying less, cooking more of our German favorites, veiner schnitzel, spaetzel, noodle puddings, and apple dumplings. She is cleaning, polishing and organizing our apartment every day. She has met a neighbor woman who speaks German.

She begs me to buy a Victrola. I make the purchase the very next day. This is clearly another step in the right direction. Mother is a music lover, so she spends many hours listening to Strauss Vienesse waltzes, concert music, and opera. I take her to Radio City Music Hall, Carnegie Hall, and Yiddish theater. We go to local movies quite frequently. She reads a daily German newspaper that features serial type soap operas.

What about me, you ask? I am working very hard and actually enjoying my sales job. I love the fine fabrics and trimmings that we sell, mostly imported from Italy. I have great rapport with department and specialty store buyers and milliners around the city. I dress immaculately in dark suits, white shirts with starched collars and tie. I wear a Fedora hat each day just like every other businessman.

I meet up with my old friend Jakob for a drink and dinner every now and then. He is a salesman, too, in the ladies' garment center.

Mother and I are surviving.

My Name is Leopold, Destiny

Dearest Marion,

It is the evening of November 18th, 1934. Mother and I have finished dinner and we are sitting comfortably in the living room listening to the radio.

"Mom, are you Ok?" There is no response. Mother is suddenly slumped forward in her chair.

"Mom, what's wrong?" I run to her. I am shaking her shoulders. Holding her face in my hands, I am crying. When I feel for a pulse in her neck, I feel nothing, there is no response. Marie Sternberg, at age 68 is dead. I am 25 years old and alone.

Somehow through the fog of my sadness, I arrange for a funeral. Old uncle Max and a few neighbors attend. In a short eulogy I try to describe my mother:

I say, "My mother, Marie, was a woman deeply schooled in the Victorian tradition. She believed in principles, standards, rules of conduct, good manners, and honesty. She was generous to a fault, perhaps not frugal enough. She believed in sharing quality food and loved fine clothing. My mother, unfortunately, left this world disillusioned. She could never fully adjust to the harshness of her new life."

One thing I know for certain is that I have to leave this apartment. I call the Salvation Army and dispose of the furniture. I give the linens, china, silverware, and other household items to Uncle Max. I pack my belongings and move into the 26th Street "Y" where I will live for the next three years.

My stay at the "Y" is in many ways very pleasant. For the first time in my life, I am completely free to come and go as I please. I have free access to the gym and all related facilities. My room has a nice view of the bustling city. It is clean with daily room service. There are concerts and lectures right at the Y. I find good places to eat, including one of my favorites, The Automat. Work is going well and I see my friends a few times a week.

I am twenty-seven years old and begin to think about getting married. At the "Y" there are discussion groups, lectures, and dances for single people. So, I start to attend.

One evening, sitting at a round table discussion group, I see across from me a young woman with beautiful green- hazel eyes and soft curly brown hair. She smiles at me. Is it really me she is smiling at? Yes, I am sure of it.

Coffee and cookies are served before the dance, so I slip over to talk to her. I find out that her name is Paula Block. I notice, too, that she has a lovely slim figure. When the music starts to play in the next room, we walk in together and begin to dance. We seem to fit. She tells me sometime later that she also noticed my blue eyes and could feel my kindness.

It takes a year of courting, but we finally decide to get married. On June 12, 1937, we are married at Paula's home, 546 12th St. West New York, NJ. The wedding is attended by Paula's parents, Sarah and Hyman Block, her brother Abe Block and his wife Laura, and her sister, Fae and her husband Albert Sussman.

We spend our honeymoon in Rockaway Park.

On December 16th, 1938, our daughter Marion Ella is born. We are living in a sunny apartment in the Washington Heights-Fort Tyron section of Manhattan, on Pinehurst Ave. Our apartment faces the Hudson River.

We are happy.

Husband Bob

Threads hold a marriage together,
hundreds of tiny threads, which sew people
together through the years. *- Simone Signoret*

When I am weak you can be strong.
When I am strong you can be weak.
That's what marriage is. *- Gisele Bundchen*

The Prickly Pear

My love is a prickly pear
He has two kinds of spines to protect
The large, smooth and fixed, in place for
stubbornness
The small hair-like prickles
that easily penetrate the skin
with which to make his mark
But, Oh, inside is the sweet succulent fruit
And the intoxicating liqueur

Nantucket Magic, Part One

Joan on left, Marion on right

Joan and I are about to dock at the Nantucket Island pier.
It is early morning July 4th weekend,1963. The sun is shining
on the sparkling Atlantic. Our ferry ride has been fun, even boisterous, with people singing, already drinking beer, and children
running around. The water remains calm so no one gets seasick.
A good omen.

As we approach the pier we are waving along with everyone else at the waiting crowd. No one is there to greet us but we wave anyway. People appear to be so friendly.

"Look at this place Joan, it's perfect. Everyone seems so nice. Do you have the directions?"

"Here's the map, it actually shows Chrisman's Cottages. It's right down the street."

We love our new cottage and quickly meet more young people who tell us about the great parties planned for the weekend.

"Parties start early here, around three o'clock," says a pretty little dark-haired young woman. "It's only Friday and there'll be parties every night till Monday when everyone catches the ferry back."

"This is our first time on Nantucket."

"You're going to fall in love here. There is magic on this Island."

It's late afternoon and Joan and I are prepping to go out. I am primping and fussing with my newly highlighted hair.

"I hate my hair!" I snarl.

"Stop it Marion. You look fine, don't worry about it. Let's just go."

In our favorite shorts, tee-shirts and flip flops, we prepare to walk down to the party house. At the last minute, I decide to change into my gold, embroidered Greek shirt.

I am nervous about meeting new people at this strange party. I am sneezing non-stop as we reach the doorway. Apparently, my allergies have followed me all the way to Nantucket. My nose is running.

Standing inside the door is a tall, tan, dark-haired young man. I notice that under his tee-shirt and shorts he is strong. I don't get as far as the flip flops.

"Do you have a tissue?" I beg.

"Wow, little girl, you come with me. I'll take you to the bathroom for the softest toilet paper on the island. I have allergies too. By the way, my name is Bob."

Rock and Roll music plays softly, as my friend Joan drifts off to talk to another tee-shirted shorts and flip flops guy.

Bob and I talk continuously about allergies, music, family and the colleges we recently graduated from.

It is 5:30 and the night is young. Bob suggests that Joan and I join him at his parent's house for a drink and a bite to eat.

"Are you sure they won't mind?"

"I'll just give them a call and let them know we're coming."

We are greeted with handshakes and hugs by Bob's parents. Don't get the wrong idea about this friendly family. They are summer residents, yes. But they are not the uppity rich, fancy house, summer people you might expect.

Murray, the dad, is a musician. He plays piano and accordion with his band at the yacht club. These people are the help. Murray is dark-haired, young looking, handsome and sweet. Florence, too, I judge to be in her mid-forties, with beautiful green eyes and the kind of creamy olive skin that tans so well. Bob has a younger sister, Annette.

On this first meeting, Florence introduces us to her drink of choice, vodka and cranberry juice. I can hardly keep up. Joan and I are getting tipsy. We are served snacks and several more drinks.

"Have another, have another! It's the Nantucket drink."

My anxiety gone, I feel a smile on my face as I look across the room at Bob who is smiling broadly back. Inside I feel a lovely, strange numbness.

Can this be love?

By 6:30 two more band members show up. Tony, the drummer is here on the Island without his wife who is back in Boston. He is quite gorgeous in a Dean Martin sort of way. He is accompanied by Tommy, the saxophone player. Tommy is a short, stocky, friendly man who is here for the summer with his wife. We are introduced all around. Dean Martin immediately takes a shine to Joan.

Uh Oh!

"Murray, Florence," Tony blurts, "the Lobster bake is going strong at the Jetties Beach. I have enough tickets for all of us. Want to go?"

"Marion, Joan, want to go? You'll love it." Bob describes how there are deep pits in the sand where lobsters, clams, scallops, corn, and even cornbread are baked on hot charcoal.

"It's fun and delicious. The beer is free and the tickets are already paid for."

So, we grab blankets and sand chairs and head to the beach. It's a jovial group. There are big bonfires. Everyone is eating and drinking. The food is the best I have ever tasted. We are dipping our lobster and clams into melted butter, licking our fingers, and drinking beer.

The sun is setting and people are playing guitars and singing. Bob and I sit alone on a blanket.

"Marion, this is the weirdest thing. We just met and yet I feel so close to you. It's kind of magical."

"I feel it too. We're having so much fun together. It has been the most incredible day." We lean into each other and kiss. It is the sweetest, tastiest kiss I have ever had.

By chance, I look over at a blanket further back on the beach.

Oh no. Are that Joan and Tony? They are laying down facing each other, first giggling, then laughing hysterically. *Oh, God, now they're kissing. It's not my business, right?* But I feel so peculiar about it.

I tell Bob.

"Joan and Tony are making out," I whisper. "What should we do?"

"Nothing at all. It's a bit of an adventure for both of them. There's no harm. It's the magic of Nantucket."

"But he's married!"

"People fall in love on this island."

"I hope you're right. Joan tends to fall in love too easily. She's a bit naive."

Joan is twenty-three, barely out of college. This guy is probably pushing fifty. It doesn't seem right.

But I let it go.

It's dark now and my watch shows 11:00. The time has flown by.

"I think we should go, it's been a long day," I hesitate to say.

Bob and I fold up our blanket and wave to Joan and Tony.

"Let's go!"

Reluctantly they follow us back to our cottage. We all kiss and hug each other goodnight. As Joan and I gently shut the door, our giggles turn to shrieks of laughter.

We are such bad girls.

For the next two days the four of us revel in the sunshine, our skin glowing, perhaps too much. We swim in the clear waters, ride bicycles all over the island, eat seafood dinners and drink wine.

On Sunday morning Bob and I are standing next to each other on the beach. We are in our bathing suits looking out at the ocean. When I look down, I suddenly notice that Bob has two webbed toes.

"Oh my God, you have webbed feet," I scream. "What does this mean?"

"It's why I'm such a good swimmer." He laughs. "It's inherited. If we get married our children might have webbed toes too."

"Married, what are you talking about?"

"Marion, this has been such an incredible weekend for me. I can't believe you're leaving tomorrow."

"For me too. I know we live far from each other but we can get together again."

"We'll work it out. I can visit you in NYC, and you can come down to Washington."

I am teaching fifth grade in New Rochelle, NY and Bob is working at the National Institutes of Health in Bethesda, Maryland.

Too soon Joan and I have to leave the Island.

Once again, we are waving to the people on the dock. This time we wave goodbye to Bob and Tony.

Bob and I know we will meet again.

Joan and Tony will not meet again, but the memory will be worth it.

1963

Surfside

(L to r) Bob, Murray, Florence, Annette, around Marion

Nantucket Magic, Part Two

It's August 28th,1963 and Bob and I are back to Nantucket for Labor Day weekend. We are sitting on the Jetties Beach listening to Martin Luther King Jr. make his *I Have a Dream* speech on our portable radio.

"I have a dream that my four little children will one day live in a nation where they will not be judged by the color of their skin but by the content of their character."

When King ends with the words from the Negro spiritual we are both feeling emotional.

"Free at last, Free at last, Great God a-mighty, We are Free at last."

Bob turns to me teary-eyed.

"This speech gives me hope but also makes me understand how short life is. You never know what will happen next."

We have been saying words of love for the last weeks. But still, I am a bit shocked when Bob speaks.

"This is crazy but Instead of all this traveling back and forth, let's get married. What do you think?"

I am surprised and excited. Why not? It is quite amazing, that we have only just met July 4th, have seen little of each other, and are now talking about marriage.

"Wow! Why not. What fun! Wow! Sure, Yes!"

With little time to really think about it, our decision sets off a whirlwind of events leading up to our wedding day, four months later. We are to be married on December 8th,1963. There will be get-togethers with our parents, showers, bachelor parties and wedding plans.

First, I have to meet Bob's grandma, Bella, who lives in a nursing home in Boston. The home is in a wooden frame house on a tree-lined street. I am nervous and wonder what she will think of me. After all, Bob is her favorite.

We arrive on a sunny September day. A nurse leads us to a large room where several old people sit in wheelchairs. Bella is a tiny, gray, withered old woman.

She looks up and seems surprised but smiles at Bob.

"Grandma, this is Marion, the girl I'm going to marry."

Bella studies me for a long time with small, sharp, crow-like eyes.

She squints and in a husky voice says, "You got a Pall Mall?"

Bob and I burst out laughing and in turn, give grandma a hug.

"Sorry Grandma, smoking is not allowed here."

With a toothless grin, she quips, "Damn!"

An elaborate shower has been arranged by my mother-in-law to be, Florence, at the Bell House in Sharon, Massachusetts. There are thirty-seven women, Bob's sisters and of course my mother and me. We have driven down from NYC together in my little Renault Caravelle.

A lovely filet of sole stuffed with crab meat is served. Murray, my father-in-law, is playing sweet 40s tunes on the piano. He has actually brought along his trio to entertain us. Mom and I get along nicely with all the women. We suffer through opening lots of presents and gifts, most of which are unnecessary. I do, however, love the "Fahbaware, complete set."

"Fahbaware, Farbaware!" the women scream.

"We love Fahbaware!"

"Thank you so much for this. I love to cook."

Toward the end of the afternoon, Mom and I are preparing to leave. I approach a large, squawking, laughing, gathering of women. Florence is standing at the center. I slide in and speak above the din.

"Florence, thank you so much for this wonderful party. Mom and I had so much fun."

Suddenly silence. The women circle around me, fluttering like chickens, with large eyes and open mouths. Each of them screeching. "What?"

"What did you say?"

"Florence? You called your mother-in-law-to-be Florence?"

"That's not right," another yells.

"You have to call her mom!"

"Let me hear you call her mom."

Florence grins nervously. My face is a burning fire. I do as I am told.

"Hi mom!"

I approach and we hug, both giggling with anxiety.

From then on I never call my mother-in-law anything.

My own mom and I pile all the silver plate, Corningware, Farberware and Tupperware into the red Caravelle and drive the six hours back to New York. I must confess we share a lot of good laughs on the trip home.

We also agree that Bob is the perfect guy for me.

Nantucket Magic, Part 3 The Wedding

On our wedding day, we feel lucky to awake to a beautiful sun, in spite of the forecast for snow.

It is December 8, 1963.

My stomach jitters and my heart flutters in a good way. All preparations have been made. I love my wedding gown, I love the venue, a contemporary synagogue in New Rochelle, and I love the man I am about to marry. My parents are jittery too. They have worked so hard to make this a perfect day for me and Bob.

True to form they stay in the background, quietly checking on details. They prepare to arrive early to greet guests as they trickle in.

Bob and I have carefully chosen our best man, matron of honor, ushers and bridesmaids. They include my cousin Marcia, my best friend Joan and Bob's middle sister, Linda.

In the little "brides room" my attendants and I are hanging out. I sit facing the mirror. Florence appears at the door smoking a cigarette.

"Oh, Marion, you look so pretty."

"Don't you love her dress?"

"It's just beautiful."

Florence is blowing smoke into the tiny room and flicking ashes on the floor. I begin to cough. With her free hand, she is primping my veil. Her next flick sends a spark from her cigarette straight to the veil. A black hole is immediately visible.

I am angry. Hot tears well up and threaten to ruin my makeup. Best friend Joan, with clenched teeth, leans toward mother-in-law.

"Florence please wait outside."

"I'm so sorry. I just like to help." She slips out, but I feel her presence. Smoke continues to waft its way under the door.

I am thinking, it's not too late to run. I can just leave. My Renault Caravelle is waiting right outside, to be used for our getaway later. But, no, I am breathing deeply. I can do this. We open the door for air. Florence is standing right there, continuing to smoke. I take some more deep breaths and proceed to give my gifts to each bridal attendant, lovely gold chains with delicate hearts at the center.

By now the guests are seated in the pews. My mom will walk down the aisle with Bob's best man and my father waits for me to take his arm, for the last mile. He looks shaky and ashen. It is time for the wedding party to line up. *Try to Remember,* our favorite from The Fantastiks begins to play. Dad and I both shake and shed tears as we walk down the aisle. I am saved when I see Bob's broad shoulders and broader smile as he watches me approach.

We are so happy.

The actual ceremony is a blur. Later, at the reception, I relax. All that matters is the love that is in this room. Surrounded by family, friends and the man I love makes it so worth it.

We all dance and sing to my father-in-law's amazing band. College friends join at the microphone and sing our alma mater.

"Marion, this is the best wedding I've ever been to."

"This food is incredible."

"You guys look so happy!"

At the right time, Bob and I slip away to change our clothes and ready ourselves to leave. We want to get away without all the delayed goodbyes.

When we step outside we are faced with the blizzard of '63. It is midnight and the snow has accumulated in drifts. The wind howls.

We push our way into my tiny Renault Caravelle. Bob frantically brushes the windows with the hope of removing at least some of the snow that is piled high.

As we take off I suddenly realize that I forgot to have the windshield wipers fixed. *Oh God! How will we be able to see?* There is not another car on the road, not even a snowplow. Visibility is zero.

We will not be deterred. This is our moment, our great escape. Bob the hero, stops every few minutes along the way to exit the car and wipe off the windshield. We keep the windows open as if it might help.

The trip from New Rochelle to Manhattan takes over three hours. When we finally arrive at the New Yorker Hotel we are soaking wet and exhausted.

As we cuddle and giggle in bed we feel a very real sense of freedom. In a few days, we will move into our new apartment in Washington, D.C. We are on our own, with no family or friends around.

"Free at last, Free at last, Thank God almighty we are free at last."

I must confess I am very happy.

Marion and Annette

Coffee

Washington, D.C. 1964, just married:

"Sweetheart, did you make coffee?"
"Darling, I'm just about to. I'm going to use our new Far-berware electric percolator. The one we got as a wedding gift from Aunt Fae."
"Great, honey, you know me, I can't function without my cof-fee." Bob likes his coffee strong and black. I love it with half and half and sugar. The pleasing aroma of Maxwell House wafts straight to our nostrils.
"Here love, I poured you a cup in your favorite mug."
"Thanks hon. Love you."

Coffee has been enjoyed around the world for hundreds of years. In France, as early as 1710 the infusion brewing process was introduced. It involved submerging ground coffee, enclosed in a linen bag, in hot water.
More than the taste, coffee lovers have always looked forward to the kick.

Boston, Massachusetts, 1970, two babies later:

"Hon, did you make coffee?"
"Yes, dear, I'm trying out our new CorningWare coffee maker. Tell me if you like this Chock full o' Nuts."
Kids screaming in the background.
"Just pour mine into the thermos. I'm late for work."
"OK, Bob, have a great day."
"You too."

Vacuum brewers, invented in 1840, were made for commercial use. Percolators were developed in the mid 19th century as well. At first, they were heated up on the stove. It was fun as a child to watch the sweet-smelling brown liquid gurgle up in the little glass dome. The electric percolator was a boon to the industry. By the early 1970s, the electric drip coffee maker was introduced and percolator sales plummeted.

Lawrenceville, New Jersey, 1983, kids in school, mom working:

"Marion, did you make coffee?"

"I'm working on it. I'm waiting for a pot of water to boil so I can use the new glass drip coffee maker. The stupid filter keeps folding and the grinds get into the coffee."

"It's getting late and I need to go. Why don't you use the Mr. Coffee you just bought?"

"Why don't you make your own damn coffee?!!"

An electric drip coffee maker can also be referred to as a dripolator. It works by admitting water from a cold water reservoir into a flexible hose leading to a heating chamber. Pressure moves the heated water into the brew basket and the coffee drips down into the glass pot. Easy. Yummy.

Lawrenceville, 1994, kids graduated college and moved away:

"Marion, I'm trying to make coffee in the French press. So I grind the beans a little coarser, right?"

"Bob, this is your baby, but I know you have to place the coffee and hot water together in the glass pot and stir. Leave it to brew for a few minutes and then press the plunger to trap the coffee grounds. I have to leave. I'm going to get mine at Dunkin Donuts. Bye."

"OK, Bye."

Lawrenceville, New Jersey, 2014, grandkids expected:

Lots of cooking and baking.

"Bob, will you throw an Italian Roast into the Keurig for me?"

"Sure, hon. I was just about to make a Green Mountain Hazelnut for myself. Don't you love it? What would we do without our coffee?"

"I don't know. I'll still take Starbucks any day of the week!"

Ou Sont Les Toilette?

"Bob, everyone says we need to bring our own rolls of toilet paper to Europe."

"Everyone? Who's everyone?"

"Well, you know, Harold and Maude and the Donnelly's have been there."

"I can't believe they don't have toilet paper in the countries we're going to. After all, it's 1964. These are civilized people."

"Well how about we each bring one roll in our backpacks?"

"Okay, but one roll each won't last for the six weeks we'll be gone."

"They must have supermarkets there. We can buy some for the car."

"I'm so excited. I'm glad we're doing this all on our own. Of course, we'll have Frommer's, *Five Dollars a Day*, and our new Peugeot. How can anything go wrong?"

"We can only hope. I'm excited too. It'll be great."

Our plan is to pick up our new car in Paris. We will travel to six countries. First, Paris, France. Then to Switzerland. Next to Italy, including Milan, Florence, Rome, and Venice. From Venice, we'll journey north to Salzburg, Austria, then to Munich, Cologne and Heidelberg Germany. We'll end up in Amsterdam and Rotterdam. That's where we'll put our car on the ship bound for Baltimore.

We are so young, so full of enthusiasm, so naive.

We arrive in Paris, tired but happy. Our taxi driver is grouchy and refuses to respond to our broken French. We don't care, as we drive by open-air meat markets, bread and flower vendors and pastry shops. We leave our windows open to absorb the aromas. It's Paris after all!

The driver slams on his brakes as we come to an abrupt stop in front of the Peugeot dealer. We give what we hope is the correct number of francs. The driver speeds away.

We love the shiny new steel gray car with actual leather seats. We hop in ready for anything. Bob at the wheel, jerks the car into first gear, forces it into second as we slowly bounce along toward the circle at the Arc de Triumph. He never gets it into third.

As we round the circle, we are suddenly caught in a screaming frenzy of cars honking, contorted faces yelling at us from their car windows. Some are giving us the finger.

"Fuck you Americans."

"Get un Cheval!"

How do they know who we are?

Welcome to Paris.

Exhausted, we find our hotel on the left bank appropriately called La Parisienne. We follow our concierge, Jacques, up the narrow flight of stairs to the top floor. There is immediately something sexy about this hotel.

Jacques is showing us our room. It is so French with it's red, fringed Tiffany chandelier, a purple satin bed cover with a peacock feather pattern and a large bolster pillow. The windows are shutters, no glass or screens. Opening them, we look out onto a typical Parisian patisserie and feel the cool breeze. A yellow and black bee buzzes on the window sill.

Just a minute. Where is the bathroom? I see a sink, but that's all.

"Jacques, ou sont le toilettes?"

"Oh, mademoiselle et monsieur, zee toilette? Zat is down zee hall."

Bob amenably says, "No problem, monsieur."

"And Jacques, where is zee shower?"

"Oh, zat is down zee other hall."

No problem? I am not so sure. No matter, I will adjust.

The sun is dipping low in the sky. It is time for dinner.

We find a charming little restaurant right on our street.

We eat Coq Au Vin and Algerian couscous. It becomes our habit to order "deux vin rouge" with every meal. We drink several. This is the best wine I have ever tasted.

We are happily drunk as we walk back to the hotel, arm in arm. The streets at midnight are still busy with other young revelers.

We are in love.

At 3:00 a.m, I need a trip to "zee toilette" right down zee hall-way. I open our door and step into pitch darkness. I am stumbling slowly feeling my way along the wall. As I try to adjust to the shadowy blackness, I see a dim light coming from under a door. That must be it.

Oh, my God, the bathroom door is locked. I hear a loud flush. The door opens and there stands a gray-haired man, pulling up his boxer shorts. We both involuntarily scream.

"Pardon, mademoiselle."

Without a reply, I push by him and quickly slam and bolt the door. I am shivering violently as I sit down. The toilet paper is brown paper, newspaper quality. Why didn't I bring my precious roll? Standing again I am dizzily leaning against the wall for sup-port. I am looking for a way to flush. I finally notice the wood han-dle of the pull chain. A lovely gush of water.

I slither back down the hall and slip into bed. Bob is snoring pleasantly.

A bee is buzzing somewhere in the room. I sleep soundly.

I will come to realize that in Europe,1964, plumbing is still somewhat primitive, try very primitive.

Lucky are the times we find pull chains.

Crash

I hear the approaching thunder, that one day will destroy us too.
I feel the suffering of millions and yet, when I look up at the sky,
I somehow feel that everything will change for the better.
—Anne Frank, 1944

Hitler's Eagles Nest, Berchtesgaden Germany, summer, 1964.

"So Marion, do you want to go to Berchtesgaden or not?"
"I am so conflicted about going. Munich has been so much fun, so welcoming, so safe. I'd hate to ruin the good feelings I'm starting to have about Germany."
"Let's just head in that direction, it's on our way to Salzburg anyway. The views of the Alps will be spectacular."
"Okay Bob, but I feel queasy and frightened just thinking about it. It was Hitler's Eagle's Nest after all. It's where he caroused with Eva Braun, even had her sister's wedding party there. I can picture all the men, Himmler and Goering, degenerates, cavorting and plotting new methods of torture and murder."

The sign reads: *Tourists Must Leave Cars at Bottom of Hill.* Hitler's Eagle's Nest can only be reached by a steep walk or the elevator which itself can only be reached by a long, damp and dark tunnel.
"Let's take the elevator."
It's a huge, cold steel box.
"I feel chilled and frightened already."
"Don't worry, all that's history now."
"Is it?"
We step outside into the glaring morning sunlight. Other tourists are milling around an outdoor cafe. They are all blond and German. Are they Nazis? Nazi sympathizers? We step to the railing to see the spectacular view.

I feel dizzy. We are eye level with the jagged mountains of the Alps which jut out in all directions. On this rare sunny day, the view is truly spectacular. We can almost see Salzburg, Austria.

The guided tour is fascinating. We are shown the massive rooms with their granite walls, heavy beamed ceilings, and large dark furnishings.

"This place was built for Hitler so he could show off to dignitaries and impressionable guests. Eva Braun entertained friends here. As a matter of fact, she spent more time here than Hitler. When he came here he felt safe, less paranoid."

We enter a room with a monstrous red marble fireplace. It was a gift from Mussolini.

The tour is ending and Bob reminds me, "We should be getting on the road, so we can get to Salzburg before dark."

I am happy to leave and feel secure once again back on the road. We are driving through the Alps when it starts to drizzle.

By now Bob and I are three weeks into our journey through Europe. We have eaten breads and cheeses. We have drunk wines. We will always remember the people we met, the music we heard, the unique beauty of each country. And each funny, edgy mishap.

But now we are tired, a bit testy, and somewhat annoyed with each other. It doesn't take much for me to get fussy and irritated. Today, I am concerned with the way Bob drives these threatening Alpine roads. I admit he is a practiced and fearless driver.

But why does he have to floss his teeth en route? He is placing his elbows on the steering wheel as his fingers glide the floss forward and back between his teeth.

"What are you doing?" I scream. "Can't you see the road is wet? Do you want to get us killed?"

"I don't know what's with you Marion, but you're getting on my nerves."

"Getting on YOUR nerves?" I screech. "You and your weird habits have been annoying me for days."

It is raining now and the Austrian road is steeper and windier. To our right is the mountain, with a deep gully. To the left is a cliff. No guardrail. Although the day is cool and humid, I am sweating and shaky.

I fantasize about divorce.

My reverie is interrupted by Bob's concern.

"I think we're a bit lost. Marion, hand me the map."

He opens the map and holds it against the steering wheel, reading it and sneaking glances at the road. We are driving at 45 mph. It is raining hard and the road is slick.

When the crash comes it brings a flash of light to my eyes. There is a loud crack and roar as we roll to the right into the ditch. The car turns on its side before it stops. We have both been thrown against the passenger side door.

A momentary silence.

Then I'm crying.

In a whisper, Bob says, "Are you okay?"

"I think so." A whimper. Then silence.

"Are you okay?"

"I think so." For a brief moment, we clutch each other, press our heads together, kiss and hug greedily.

When we realize it is only the car that is broken, we climb out on the driver's side and look around. We are in a wilderness near an unknown Austrian village. We look up to the top of the hill and in amazement see a small boy with a basket looking down at us.

As we crawl and claw our way out of the gully the little boy remains stationary. His eyes are wide and his mouth is open.

"Zis is Zaya Schlim, very dangerous, yah?" Bob says to the boy.

"Yah, Sehr Gefafahrick." The boy looks concerned.

"Do you shprechan any English?"

"Yah, a bit. I get my Papa."

The boy scampers off, dropping some mushrooms from his basket.

What happens next comes as a surprise. It is about to become a magical, topsy-turvy, Hansel and Gretel fairy tale.

The rain has let up as we sit cross-legged on the ground waiting for something to happen. A ray of sunlight appears at the edge of the forest. It creates a kind of spotlight for the boy and his father. They are walking toward us hand in hand.

The father is wearing lederhosen with suspenders and a real Tyrolian hat. He walks with a beautifully carved walking stick. A tall man, he has a ruddy complexion and waves to us with a smile. He approaches with arms outstretched. He speaks in English.

"My boy tells me you had a bad accident. This is a terrible road. You are lucky to get away vit your life."

"We were so frightened but I think we're okay. We just don't know what we're going to do!" Bob admits.

"I can see that the front of your car is in bad shape, but ve can get it fixed tomorrow yah? You vill stay with us for the night. My Frau is a good cook and vill take care of you.

"Oh, how can we thank you enough for your help? We are so lost!" I am crying now.

"What is your name?"

"I am Jan und this is my son Hans."

"We are Bob and Marion." We shake hands.

"Now follow me to our house."

The sun is setting as we trudge through the woods to the clearing.

My Mother-in-Law and Madame de Pompadour, (Mistress of King Louis XV) Rosenthal German China

I have always enjoyed mother-in-law jokes until the day I became one.

Jokes like:

She to him: "This wine is full-bodied and imposing with a nutty base, a sharp bite, and a bitter after taste."

He to her: "Are you describing the wine or your mother?"

Or, Fred and Rick at the bar:

"Did you hear this one? A young man comes home to mom to tell her that he is in love and getting married.

"Mom, I'm going to bring over three beautiful women. I want you to guess the one I've chosen." The next day three women appear.

"So which one Mom?"

"The one on the right."

"How did you know?"

"I don't like her."

When mother-in-law Florence calls on a cold Saturday morning and speaks in a quiet, raspy voice we are worried. She is calling to ask Bob and me to meet her, in one hour, at her favorite breakfast spot, IHOP.

On the drive there we try to speculate,

"God, I hope she's not sick," Bob says,

"Maybe your dad is."

"Maybe something happened to one of my sisters. Listen, let's not assume the worst. We're almost there."

Lost in my thoughts for the next several minutes, I remember that I have forgiven Florence for burning a hole in my wedding veil with her cigarette. I forgive her yenta friends for guilting me into calling her "mom." I forgive her for always asking me if I am tired. I forgive her asking how I *caught* her son.

As we open the door we smell the undeniably scrumptious aroma of pancakes and bacon. When we feel the warmth of the room we are reassured.

We see mom sitting in the furthest booth holding a cup of coffee in both hands. I always will remember those hard-working, strong peasant hands. No fancy nail salons for her.

She is never afraid to get her hands dirty when she works in the neighborhood garden or cleans house. She works tirelessly as the head sales clerk in a women's clothing store. There, she physically lifts clothing from racks and gets on her hands and knees to create window displays. She single-handedly brings dress after dress to the dressing rooms to hard-to-please customers. She stays late after work cleaning up the messes.

Her face is grim as she looks up and sees us. Her eyes, behind her glasses, as olive-green as ever, are moist. Her flawless skin remains tan even in winter. She tries hard to smile, but all she can muster is a grimace.

"Mom, what's up? What's going on?"

"Just sit down and I'll tell you."

We wait.

"Well here goes," she begins.

"Bobby, you know that I'm not talking to your sister, Linda. Since she and her family moved to Maine, she's been constantly borrowing money from me and dad. We had to cut her off, and it made her very angry. We have not spoken in six months. You are the responsible one and have the room, so we want to give you all the Rosenthal china and Dalton silverware."

"Mom, is that all? We were so worried about you. Are you sure you want to do this? Are you that angry at Linda that you don't want her to have any of it?"

"Yes, there is no use discussing it further. I am going to have it all shipped to your house, all twelve place settings of china and silverware and accessories, all the serving pieces, everything. I want to do it immediately."

I have seen and admired this elegant china with intricate floral patterns and pure gold trim. The silver is splendid, heavy in weight with a beautiful curlicue "P" and an ornately carved rose on each piece. All of it is mostly kept in the magnificently carved, ceiling-high, cherry wood, Chippendale breakfront, which has soft, felt-lined drawers and church like glass panels.

Mostly I just peek into the cabinet and marvel at this dinnerware that seemed incongruous in their small Boston apartment. There is a beauty too, in the large dining table and carved chairs that pushed the limits of the small dining room. I have never seen the dishes used.

None of it seems to fit in a family where people talk with full mouths, where salad is grabbed with one's hands, where soup is slurped, where food is pushed onto forks by way of the thumb, and fingers are luxuriously licked off, one by one. I remember being fascinated at the way Florence stirred her vodka and cranberry juice, with her middle finger, and how Murray did the same with his scotch on the rocks. Both bouncing the ice cubes from time to time, clink, clink and suck, sucking the excess from the finger.

When it all arrives several days later it includes the breakfront as well. Our house is largely contemporary, with sleek lines and light Scandinavian woods. We make room in the dining room and are proud to call the room eclectic.

Now I have time to really take a look. Every piece of hand-painted Rosenthal, Pompadour, German china is different. At first glance, I see thick gold trim and luscious flowers; roses, irises, bluebells, and purple daisies. To my surprise, on some bowls and plates, these flowers are just buds, while some are in half bloom. Sometimes there appear flowers in full bloom. Each dish is an amazing work of art. The china is so fine that you can feel the silky-smooth surface and the delicately raised hand-painted flowers.

Interesting too is the variety of dishes. Each place setting has a large plate, a soup bowl, a bread and butter plate, a salad plate and a dessert dish. The sterling silverware has many utensils in each place setting, not to mention all the serving pieces.

What am I going to do with all of this?

I know that you are supposed to start a meal using silver from the outer piece and work your way inward. The butter knife is to be placed above the plates. A diner would start with the soup

138

spoon, move on to the salad fork, then the dinner fork and knife, finally the small spoon and fork for dessert. Why does this family care to have such finery?

God bless them. I suppose it is all about dreams and aspirations, the dream world of the poor. This gives the immigrants who arrive in America the promise of better things to come. These people take pride in collecting and saving these elegant treasures for posterity. Some, I presume had been given as wedding gifts, some purchased over the years. Here we are now possessors of rewards for all the decades of hard labor.

What a generous gift.

It is given with love.

It has been more than thirty years since we received this gift. We do from time to time use it all for dinner parties and holiday celebrations. Mostly our grown children Jonathan and Susan make fun of it all. Why the opulence? What are you trying to prove? Why would grandma want such fancy dishes and silver?

I explain the history and psychology to them and say, "Well, it will all be yours, someday."

"We don't want it!" they reply, in unison.

Our youngest grandson Gabriel pipes up.

" I really like it Grandma. I think it's beautiful. Will you save it for me?"

Mom on left, Florence, Bob's mother, on right

This Too Shall Pass

As time passes I notice that Florence adds a touch of grapefruit juice to her vodka and cranberry juice, in an ever-larger glass.

"It's a Sea Breeze. Want one?"

"Sure!" I say. Although it is hard to keep up, I manage to always get a nice buzz at our family gatherings, enjoying the usual hilarity in the room. Bob, on the other hand, only drinks beer.

"Mom, get me any beer except Miller. I hate Miller." Every time we visit, Bob is handed a Miller.

It is hard to say at what point Florence goes from forgetfulness to dementia. It is certainly after Murray dies. It is slow but noticeable. Along with it comes anxiety and aggressiveness. The diagnosis is dementia, probably Alzheimers Disease.

As she becomes more agitated she will say things like, "What did you do to catch my amazing son Bobby?" I get into the habit of laughing everything off. I know she loves me. I am always kind to her and call her once a week.

Burned forever in my mind is the day we put Florence in the nursing home. She has been living in a beautiful assisted living apartment. It is new and modern on two levels. She has invited to dine twice a day in the sparkling dining room.

We begin to get calls complaining about her behavior with the other residents. Apparently, she approaches and pinches or hits them.

She yells, "Why don't you talk to me?"

"When will you be my friend?"

"I want to sit with you."

Here is a woman who, all her life, has been a good friend, who has wonderful female companions, who now is being shunned by her peers. No one wants to be seen with her. She is too loud, they say, she insults everyone. She no longer can filter her thoughts and feelings. The social worker finally asks us to find a more suitable place for her.

After an extensive search, we find Swaying Pines nursing home. We tell mom that we are going to show her a new place to live. On that day we are a band of six. Bob and I, our children Susan and Jon, Bob's sister, Annette, and mom.

We all go out to lunch and then on to the home. It is quite lovely, but the residents are old, many in wheelchairs with mouths that hang open. Florence still seems young and strong. We find a room where a piano player is playing Frank Sinatra tunes and Florence begins to sing along. Soon I and the children disappear and leave the hard part to Bob and Annette.

"Mom, we're going to leave you here for a few days to see how you like it."

Not surprising, Florence cries, "This is where you're putting me?"

"Just try it out," they say, and leave her.

Of course, she never does leave. She begins to adjust and gets along rather well with the nurses and social workers. She continues to be hostile to the residents, but the heavy medication helps. In the end, she barely knows us, but she is able to use the cliches she has accumulated through the years. Although she doesn't remember our names she laughs and shouts in her Boston accent.

"Hi, how ah ya?" She is always so happy to see us. In conversation, she knows all the idioms.

"Oh well, tomorrow is another day."

"That's life."

"Better safe than sorry."

Finally, near the end, she keeps repeating her favorite.

"This too shall pass."

The Rap Group

We know that the Sexual Revolution of the sixties really happened in the seventies. It started for me in1964 when I read *Diary of a Mad Housewife*, by Sue Kaufman, and *The Feminine Mystique,* by Betty Friedan.

My mother, who was born in 1900, worked for women's voting rights. She saw her efforts reach fruition in 1920. She was my role model. So the seeds were sown early.

In the late sixties and early seventies when the Beatles were all the rage, their music deeply resonated with us. We listened to every word and loved each note. If you walked by our open window you might hear *Long and Winding Road* from the 1970s *Let it Be* album or tunes from *Abbey Road.* I began to walk down a road we called *freedom.*

In 1974 our children Jonathan and Susan were ages eight and six. Bob and I had been married for eleven years. I was thirty-six years old.

It is no surprise I was attracted to the women's movement. My best friend Barbara introduced me to Liz who was a well-known NOW leader, the National Organization of Women, in Princeton. Her South African charm, deep knowledge of the subject and welcoming charisma helped me to say "Yes," when she invited us to a conscientious raising meeting.

She explained, "Marion, the group is just getting underway, we meet once a week in different women's houses. You will add so much." As it turned out three of my friends were going to participate as well.

I felt anxious during that first meeting. I entered a strange living room and was welcomed by a woman I did not know.

"Come on in Marion. Grab a glass of wine and join us!"

I looked around to see a room full of women, of all ages, sitting in a circle. Liz was leading the group. She was explaining what consciousness-raising was about.

"We will look at history and the ways women were subjugated. We will realize how we always played the role of servant to men, for centuries. Our salaries have never been equitable. We could

143

not own property or cars. I want to remind you that even now women are being shut out of jobs that only men can hold. Open to us are teacher, nurse or secretary jobs. We women have been the child-rearers, the cooks and toilet cleaners. Men have had the power."

She stopped but then continued.

"This has got to stop. We will find ways to improve our lives and fight for our rights. The group is strictly confidential. Here you can feel free to tell your own stories of abuse and subjugation."

It was an awakening that I had not expected. I had gripes about who controlled the money in our family—my husband. I was aware of who did all the cooking and cleaning and a good deal of childcare, not to mention my part-time job.

The wife, me! I had been feeling under-appreciated and over-worked. But I was afraid to admit that for the most part life was good.

During that first meeting, everyone helped themselves to white or red wine, which sat in large bottles on the kitchen table. They thought drinking would help us to open up and to share real-life experiences and secrets.

What stories I heard. I mostly listened, giggled, whooped with pleasure or gasped in horror. The meeting ended at 11:30 p.m. I walked the distance home with my friend, elated, empowered and drunk.

Ten to fifteen women showed up each week. Ages ranged from twenty-five to fifty-five. Everyone was Caucasian with different ethnic backgrounds. Some were married with children, some without and several singles. We were all college-educated and well-read. Stories ranged from the damage mothers had done, to verbal abuse by fathers, to terrible marriages to either weak or domineering husbands. In each session, we tried to find ways to evoke change, to share ideas about sharing household burdens and to better get along with family members.

Some ideas for creating change were:

"Cooking for the family ends tomorrow. It's take-out from now on."

"I'm not going to clean the bathrooms anymore."

"I'm going on strike."

"I am going to do more away from home." We planned a retreat for the near future.

One time, besides wine, some members brought marijuana.
"Let's smoke a joint tonight and see where it takes us."
"Smoking *grass* will help us see our lives more clearly."
"Yeah, and help us think more creatively."
I began to feel a bit uneasy, but was in it for the long term so was willing to take part. Fortunately, I had a ride home with a friend who refused to smoke. I was very high, happy and hungry when I got home at midnight. Bob and the children were asleep. I slipped into the shower to wash away the odor of wine and marijuana and tiptoed into bed, head spinning.

So it continued.

A year later we were still an active group. It became clear that many women agreed it was necessary, in order to become truly liberated, that you needed to have an affair and get a job. I went from my part-time job to full time!

It was easy to get back into teaching. My children were in school all day and I was welcomed back to teach a 6th-grade class at Dutch Neck School.

What lingered, however, was the growing discontent in our marriage. Bob resented the time I spent with these women. He was hurt and felt abandoned when I went on weekend retreats with them.

"Why do you have to do this? You have responsibilities at home."

He had to take care of the children and do household tasks while I was gone. This made him angry. Also, all the husbands and significant others wondered what we talked about.

"Do you talk about me at these meetings?"

It was inevitable that some meetings were at my house. Sometimes when I hosted Bob would go to meetings of his own or work late. On one of these nights, he was home upstairs reading. His door was shut and I thought he was asleep.

There was one young woman in the group, named Betty Jane, who was only twenty-four years old. She had pretty, very long, straight black hair that she wore loose. She let it swish into her face when she looked down. She was an arch-feminist, a heavy drinker and a smoker. She told us stories of her dabbling with other drugs as well.

"It's so weird, but every time a meet a man I like, I think it's my obligation to go to bed with him," she shared.

"Betty Jane, It seems as though you're giving up your hard-fought freedom too easily. Where is your fight for autonomy?"

Betty Jane only shrugged and swished her hair into her eyes. Our meeting that night went on for hours, with wine and indignation to sustain us.

At 11:45 I heard stomping on the stairs. Bob suddenly appeared in his plaid boxer shorts and tee-shirt.

Everyone turned to look.

"Ladies, the party is over now. It's time you all went home. I need to get some sleep," he yelled.

"We just need a few minutes to finish up," I said.

"No, you don't. I am asking you all to leave now! This is my house!" His face was red with anger. He trudged back up the stairs.

Everyone got up slowly. Each woman hugged and kissed me goodnight as they slinked out the door.

"I am so sorry!"

Betty Jane was the last to leave. She was obviously quite wasted. She whispered in my ear.

"He's really cute, I could go for him."

Children

Children have never been very good at listening to their elders, but they have never failed to imitate them. — *James Baldwin*

Be nice to your kids.
They choose your nursing home. — *Phyllis Diller*

When my kids become wild and unruly, I use a nice safe playpen. When they're finished I climb out. — *Erma Bombeck*

Susan and Jonathan

La Leche

In 1966 childbirth still remains a private matter between obstetricians and mothers-to-be. Husbands are not invited into the delivery room. Fine with me. The thought of having any hovering, shrieking extended family, even Bob, staring at my business is unthinkable. Bob is just as happy to pace with the other dads in the waiting room. There are no Lamaze classes, no lactation specialists. Breastfeeding is largely considered Third World.

Living in Washington, D.C. I find a group of doctors who are on the "cutting" edge. They believe in epidurals and episiotomies. They are also advocates of breastfeeding.

When my water breaks at 9:00 p.m. on August 14th after eight months of pregnancy, I am told to go to the hospital. Bob helps me pack a bag and we drive to George Washington University Hospital. Contractions come regularly.

I will be forever grateful to their wonderful nurses and the amazing anesthesiologist.

"I am going to insert a tiny tube into your spine which will administer lovely numbing medicine. It's called an epidural. But if your contractions stop, we will have to stop the flow." He pats my belly and leaves the room.

I am alone except for a nurse who peeks in every once in a while.

I relax and watch the rise of my abdomen with each contraction. No pain.

I am so grateful.

At 2:00 a.m. my doctor arrives, checks me, and says, "You are ready to go to the delivery room."

When I am all set up the doctor says, "You can push now."

"Okay, but what do you mean, push?"

He replies with a giggle, "The way you move your bowels!"

"Oh! Okay." I obey.

At 2:13 a.m. on August 15th, my baby boy is born. I watch with astonishment and giddy laughter as they lift the slippery baby from my body. He is so beautiful. Jonathan Harris Pollack weighs 5 pounds, 11 ounces.

I stay in the hospital for three nights. On the first morning, a nurse appears with my sweet little baby boy.

"You can feed him now."

My reply, "Can you just show me how?"

"Just press his little face against your breast, he will show you the way."

Many attempts later, my baby clamps on. This hurts quite a bit. I try to relax, to stay calm, to enjoy the process. After all, I have given life to this most precious child. Now I have to keep him alive. He works very hard.

He is so hungry!

When we get home my mother waits for us. She is there to help and is great with cooking, cleaning up and listening to me complain. The episiotomy is killing me. Sitz baths are recommended. The baby keeps nursing with great gusto. The problem is that he is hungry every hour. He screams and cries to be fed, yet again.

Sleep is impossible. Mom and Bob help change diapers and tend to other real-life concerns. As for feeding it is just me and baby Jon. After five completely sleepless days and nights, I call the pediatrician.

"I need help. This baby is never satisfied. He cries all the time. We are all exhausted."

His reply is unthinkable. "Give him a supplemental bottle."

"But he won't want to nurse if I do that!"

"Trust me he will."

Luckily my mother, who has been encouraging me to do just that has brought a case of already prepared bottles of, excuse the expression, formula. We crack one open. The baby drinks and drinks, guzzles, gurgles, and drinks more.

Bubbles appear at the corners of his mouth. He begins to relax. He burps. He sleeps. Relief at last. I am happy for him but troubled at the same time. I want to give our baby the very best start and that means breastfeeding for at least six months.

I have heard about the La Leche League through the mother's grapevine and have read some of their literature. The pamphlet lists a twenty-four-hour hotline number.

"Call Any Time for help."

It is late at night when I make the call. A perky voice answers. "How can we help you?" I tell my tale of woe.

"I am exhausted, sore, and so frustrated. What should I do?"

"Drink beer," she says.

"Feed him every hour and your milk will increase. And whatever you do, do not supplement or your milk will dry up!!"

"Oh, no!"

I am determined to persevere. So every hour for six more days, drunk on beer, I feed my baby. No formula.

The day comes when we have to see the pediatrician. I am so nervous because deep down I know that my baby has not gained much weight.

The doctor is not at all happy with me.

"Do you want your baby to live?"

"How can you ask such a question?"

"Well then give him a supplemental bottle after each breast-feeding."

So I do. Everyone is happy. My baby thrives.

A beer, once in a while is nice too!

Jonathan and daughter Ariel

Pretty Little Brown-eyed Susie

Brown eyes with flecks of green
my golden flower,
Susie

You rejuvenate my world
Sha la la

Little brown-eyed girl
you slip from my body easily
With baby doll silk for skin and downy little-chick hair
You cuddle and suckle lusciously at the swollen breast
Sweet fragrant dew drops on your brow

I am revived
Sha la la

Little brown-eyed girl
you waddle and toddle away
Fall on the ground
Mommy, mommy I fell down!
I won't let you fall again, come to Momma!

Pretty little brown-eyed girl growing fast, running,
riding, skating
laughing with playmates
bounce, bounce on the trampoline
jump up, up, up

My brown-eyed girl, do you remember when you left
me to run wild and free
hanging like ripe fruit with your friends?
Will you come back?
Sha la la la

A streak of blood in her bathing suit.
What is wrong with me?
You can have babies now, lucky you!
I don't want babies, I want freedom!

Hair shines long, skin glows bright,
boys notice
Brown-eyed Susie falls in love
No escaping now
Love then marriage

My brown-eyed girl swells with child. My baby
is having a baby!

Sha la la la

A Dog Named Sally, Part One

Jonathan is ten and Susan is eight. Bob, without discussing it with me, brings Sally home from the farm.

"Guess what I have here kids, your early birthday present." He is cuddling a small reddish fluffy ball of fur.

When the kids realize that this soft, fuzzy ball is a puppy, they are immediately thrilled and in love. There is no going back. My glaring, angry stares and rolling eyes at Bob go unnoticed.

For the children's sake, I lift this pup from Bob's arms.

"Aw, how sweet, so adorable, so soft."

"Her name is Sally. She was born on John's farm. It's a gift."

As I sit on the floor petting her I notice her very large paws and long tail.

"What kind of dog is this anyway?"

"Well, they told me she is mostly Golden Retriever, with some German Shepard and a bit of Saint Bernard."

Saint Bernard? The rescue dog that carries a little barrel of brandy around its neck? What does this mean? What will she become?

"Who is going to take care of her?" I question.

Everyone finally notices my concern.

"Mom, don't worry, we'll take care of her!" Jon is holding her now.

"Yeah, Mom, we'll walk her every day and feed her too." Susie is kissing the dog's face.

Right.

Neither Bob nor I have ever had a dog. We know absolutely nothing. We understand she has to be trained to do her business outside. We know she has to be fed. We know we will have to leave her alone in the house every day when we go to work and school.

"We can put up a gate in the kitchen and leave her food and water," Bob suggests. We are so hopeful, so optimistic, so stupid.

Sally grows very fast. She becomes a seventy-pound, golden, silky furred, loving dog. She loves everyone who comes her way.

She jumps up, kisses faces then nuzzles and licks their genital areas. People find her funny and adorable.

She is not adorable.

Sally has a pretty face but she is dumb. Sally does not train easily at all. Leaving her in the kitchen is a disaster. She poops and urinates, chews the cabinets, splashes water and food and knocks down the gate. She has the run of the house. She chews on furniture and clothing. She is an outdoor dog who hates being confined.

If the kids get home first, they are in charge of walking her.

"Jon, it's your turn to walk her."

"No way, Susan, I'm too busy, you do it."

We have a real problem here!

A Dog Named Sally, Part Two

When the children walk Sally she actually walks them. Susan, a petite little eight-year-old is always eager to volunteer. One morning she chooses her favorite outfit to wear to school, white duck pants and a red and black plaid shirt. Sally is jumping up and licking Susan's face as she fastens the leash. So much love.

After a while, I'm wondering why they are gone so long. Suddenly the door bursts open. Susan is crying uncontrollably. Sally is nowhere to be seen. What I notice first are the red, swollen streaks across Susan's right hand and arm. Her white pants are covered in mud.

"Mommy, Sally saw a squirrel and started to run after it." She sobs.

"Did you let go of the leash?"

"Mom, the leash was wrapped around my arm!" She is hysterical now.

"She dragged me to the creek!"

"How did you get free?" I am crying now too.

"She finally stopped for a minute and I loosened the leash."

"Oh God. I'm so sorry this happened to you."

"She's in the creek right now!" Susan wails.

"That damn dog. I hate her."

"No Mommy, don't hate her. She didn't mean it!"

Years later I learn that Susan did more than diligent duty in caring for Crazy Sally. She wiped up messes on her own, and never mentioned it. She roamed the neighborhood looking for Sally with treats to coerce her to come home. She knew that Sally was uncontrollable, but she loved her and was afraid we'd give her away.

"Here Sally, look at the treat I have for you," while Sally would play the teasing game, coming close then running away.

"Mom, can you get the car and drive around to pick her up?"

"Okay, Susan, but this is ridiculous."

Sally likes to ride in the car. She sits like a queen in the back seat, loving the breeze from the open window blowing her ears back. Jonathan sometimes worries that she seems car sick.

On this nightmare of a morning, Sally finally arrives home from the creek wet and smelly. From her mouth hangs a small mouse. She drops it at the doorway and smiles! Smiles? Can dogs smile?

We take her to the backyard, soap her up and hose her down. She is happy and relaxed. She falls asleep on the fuzzy rug in the family room. We call in late for school.

The family continues to put up with this for a while because Sally is so sweet and lovable. She never shows anger. The children can do anything to her, dress her up in clothing and costumes, ride her and cuddle up with her. It's so lovely to see them watch TV together, all piled up on the rug. This is unconditional love.

Bob becomes unhappy when our training doesn't take. All the reading about how to do it is useless. We put pepper in the garbage to dissuade her, but she loves the garbage anyway. She disdains dry dog food so we supplement her diet by adding bits of meat.

Are we too kind?

Bob puts her nose in her accidents and yells, "NO!"

She doesn't get it.

He whacks the floor with a newspaper which makes her look nervous. She doesn't get the connection.

We compliment her when she poops and pees outside. She still doesn't get it.

It is time to call Fred Fink, the famous dog trainer.

Animals who Bark, Bay, Howl, Cry, Squawk or Crow

Sally Part Three: The Subpoena

Fred Fink, the dog trainer, visits us many times to train us. He comes to our house twice a week for a month. The routine is the same. He rushes in and asks for a glass of milk for his ulcer. Sally slinks away. Work begins.

"Listen up guys, do exactly as I tell you and Sally will become a pussy cat."

A pussy cat? I hate cats.

The only other time we see Sally show fear is at the vet's. She shivers violently as we push her large body onto the table. The doctor is kind but firm and she succumbs reluctantly to his treatment. Why doesn't she succumb to us? Her other emotions include joy, excitement, and jealousy. The children hug each other on purpose just to make her nose her way between them with jealous whines and yelps.

Fred Fink teaches us how to use the choke collar and how to make Sally obey commands like sit, stay and lie down. He teaches us how to keep food out of sight. Unfortunately, it's never out of sniffing distance. Sally has a very long and wide reach with amazing ability to jump up onto counters.

Fred places an electric charge collar around her neck for the times when she refuses to obey. It is quite a harsh punishment for the poor creature and horrible to see her fly through the air when we shock her to make her come.

Bob is concerned.

"This seems like cruel punishment. Do we have to do this? We don't like this at all." But Mr. Fink promises, "It's only for a short time guys until she gets the message."

Sally begins to behave, especially when Fred is around. Everyone takes turns walking her and practicing our lessons.

"Sit, Sally, stay!"

"Lie down, Sally, good girl!"

We still have to leave Sally alone for many hours a day. We place her in an empty, good sized room upstairs, with water, food, and toys, hoping for the best. After two days we notice that she has opened the sliding closet door and shredded several of Bob's suits and family photos. We add a latch and tape the door shut. *Well, you asked for it Bob! You wanted her. You brought her home without discussing it first!!*

One day I receive a call at work from a neighbor, Lew, who cannot believe what he just saw.

"Marion, I was taking a walk and I actually just saw Sally fly out of your second-floor window. She seems okay. She landed, sprang to her feet, and is running around the neighborhood."

Sally had clawed her way through the window screen and jumped to freedom.

When we arrive home we find her waiting for us on the porch with a smile on her face. Again I ask, can dogs smile? What do I know?

We decide that she is just too big and frisky to leave alone in the house. We create a nice long run for her and a partial opening in the garage door so she can rest, eat and drink inside, and slip outdoors at her pleasure.

Things go well for a while. We think our problems are solved until we are subpoenaed. We are summoned to appear in court by the neighbors whom we have never met, who live across the street.

Bob and I go to court and see these people for the first time. They present a tape recording which the judge plays for all to hear. It starts with birds chirping but soon we hear the howls, the whines, the barks and the crying of a dog which we recognize as Sally.

Lawrence Township has just instituted a noise ordinance and we are the first to be accused. It prohibits excessive barking, baying, howling, crying, squawking or crowing. The judge scolds us but also suggests that it would have been proper for these neighbors to complain to us first.

We pay a fine of one dollar.

Now we have a real dilemma. There is an organization called APAW which takes in difficult dogs. By now I am frustrated and tired of the struggle.

I decide to call a family meeting.

At dinner, I announce, "We should consider sending Sally away."

"Mom, how can you think that? Sally is part of our family."

" Mom, how can you be so mean? Would you give one of us away?"

Bob is silent.

I am frustrated and irritated.

"Well it's me or Sally. Which is it gonna be?"

Everyone looks at each other around the table. There is complete silence.

I feel the wheels of the bus roll over me.

Tears are shed, more promises are made. Everyone agrees to try harder.

We keep Sally and I grudgingly stay.

We finally hire a dog sitter to care for Sally while we're away, taking her out for the long frolicking walks she so deserves.

With time she settles down.

Sally lives for fourteen years.

She is now a precious family memory.

Jon and Sally

160

Sally and Susan

Sally

161

Frank and Frisky

In 1976 I am still working full time at Dutch Neck School. Jonathan is ten and Susan eight. The children are beginning to understand that they are responsible for getting themselves ready and out in the morning. No more forgetting lunches or musical instruments. They are also in charge of walking Sally and feeding the gerbils, Frank and Frisky. They love the gerbils as much as they do Sally. To be on the safe side we hire Kathy, a teenager who lives next door, to babysit after school. All good right? Well....

Our children seek freedom too. When the babysitter can't come they enjoy being home alone. They watch what they want on television, eat snacks and have fun with Sally, Frank, and Frisky. They like taking the gerbils out of the Habitrail and design paper towel roll tunnels and mazes around the house. When Frank and Frisky begin to reproduce, the brood grows in number to thirty-two. This causes a problem because Sally loves to grab a baby or two for a snack.

One day I am attending a staff meeting after school and am called to the office for an urgent phone call. I am fearful that my worst nightmares are realized. I race to the phone. Naturally, it is a day that the kids are home alone. Jon's voice is shaky.

"We don't know what to do Mom. We need your help. Frank and Frisky crawled under the refrigerator and won't come out."

"Why did you let them out of the cage?"

"Because they like their freedom Mom!!" How can I argue with that?

"Okay, here's what you do. Get the broom and gently slide the stick side under the refrigerator and swish it around. I'll wait." I wait. The school secretary is rolling her eyes.

"Mom, it's not working!" He moans.

"How about putting some food in front of the refrigerator and just quietly wait there until I get home? Don't make a noise. I'll be there as soon as I can."

"Okay, Mom."

They are sitting cross-legged in front of the refrigerator when I arrive. Eventually, as evening approaches, Frank and Frisky emerge. They seem quite exhausted and happy to be put back in their cage. We are tired too by the time dad gets home. The children enjoy telling the harrowing tale.

Freedom does not come cheaply. There is always a struggle. I remember the time when the elementary school nurse calls to tell me that Jonathan is sick. I ask her to keep him in her office until I get there. She chooses to drive him home herself and he throws up in her car. She leaves my latch-key child alone on the front porch. When I arrive home Jon is quietly watching TV and drinking a Sprite.

Another time I get a call at work from the middle school nurse.

"Mrs. Pollack, Jon was on a field trip all morning. He's gotten glass in his eye. You need to come right away to take him to the doctor." I rush to get my principal to cover my class.

I race to the nurse's office. I see she has put a patch over his eye. I picture the worst.

Recklessly I drive him to the pediatrician.

"Jon, you'll be fine. Don't worry." Jon sits calmly in the back seat.

"I know Mom."

At Doctor Atkin's office, It feels like an endless wait. Jonathan stays relaxed, reading a comic book with his good eye.

I am covering my eyes as the doctor slowly removes the patch.

"Oh, no worries. It's only some mucous caused by allergies!"

What a relief. We all start laughing.

"Thank you, Doctor!"

"Thank you, God!"

Ay Ay Ay Ay

"Be sure to take plenty of cash with you," the travel agent recommends. "Your traveler's checks and credit card won't do you much good."

In 1984, Cozumel, the island off the eastern coast of Mexico's Yucatan Peninsula, has not yet become a popular resort. It's sparkling blue-green waters, with an array of colorful fish, it's soft white sands and consistently luxuriously warm weather is unknown to much of the world.

In the spring of Jon's senior year of high school, our family of four decides to take a trip to this beautiful Island. Jon, 17, Susan,15, Bob and I are excited at the prospect of this last vacation before our son goes off to college. We will fly to Cancun, then hop a small plane to paradise, the "Island of Swallows."

As always there is a last-minute flurry of activity at our house. We scurry for our passports and pack last-minute items

"Mom where is my new bathing suit?"

"Don't forget the sun lotion."

I check for my supply of antacids, anti-diarrhea meds and motion sickness pills.

We make it to the airport on time and I pop my always faithful Dramamine. The flight to Cancun is uneventful. Giddy with the sense of adventure, we disembark and feel the sudden blast of heat. In April the weather is continuously hot and sunny.

We wait an hour for our small, 20 seat plane to refuel before we can fly to Cozumel. We can see it on the tarmac through the large window. The waiting room is stuffy without air conditioning. Time passes and we notice a band of workers with tool kits surrounding the tiny airplane. We gather at the window to watch as plane parts are strewn in rows on the runway.

Finally, the announcement comes.

"Flight 26 will be delayed due to mechanical difficulties."

Welcome to Mexico.

"Mom, why is it taking so long?" whines Jon.

"Mom, I'm so hot and thirsty," groans Susan.

"Here's some money, go get something to drink," Bob placates.

Four hours later, after another Dramamine and a bumpy flight, we watch the sunset as we finally arrive in Cozumel.

We are greeted on the runway by a large Mariachi band, clad in full, red Mariachi costumes. They wear wide sombreros with fringe and tiny balls, uniforms with sparkling buttons. They welcome us with pasted grins on their faces. They play guitars and trumpets and begin to sing the ever famous Ay, Ay, Ay, Ay song, Cielito Lindo. This is the popular Ranchero song written in 1882, known to visitors all over the world.

We are staying at the one large hotel on the Island called the Mayan. It is all stucco, in the Spanish style, with exposed wooden beamed ceilings.

We reach the beach and it is sprawling, with powdery, white sand. The water is truly blue-green and the snorkeling is amazing even for me. You can merely walk into the water and float like a dead body to see an array of strikingly colorful fish.

"Mom and Dad, this is so much fun. I love it here," laughs Susan.

"Yeah, this is the best snorkeling ever. Thanks for taking us on this trip," joins Jon.

On the first day, we eat all our meals at the hotel, always sitting outside. There are chirping Emerald birds and a lazy iguana at our feet. We have been told to stay away from salads and fruit without skin but there is plenty of delicious cooked Mexican food to eat.

On the second day, we venture into the town of San Miguel. Here we begin to see the Mayan people as they go about their daily activities. There are shabby stucco buildings, crowded souvenir shops, and aggressive street vendors. Our hearts are moved by the gangs of little children hawking little boxes of Chiclets, which they sell at two for a nickel. Jon and Susan find them adorable.

"Dad, can we get some change so we can buy gum from these kids?"

We, of course, have remembered to carry cash and easily exchange a few dollars for nickels. Pesos are not necessary. This is so sweet to watch, our kids so generously purchasing Chiclets from each of the little children surrounding them. We place the candy in my big bag.

"That's it kids," giggles Susan.

"We're out of money you guys," jokes Jon.

"No kidding," barks Bob.

But the children continue to scream "Chiclet, Chiclet." They make a circle around us, grabbing at our hands and clothing. Even when we push through they continue to follow us for blocks yelling, "Chiclet, Chiclet," not satisfied, demanding more.

We escape down an alley and stop at an outdoor cafe for lunch. We have tamales and tacos and sip beers. There is a lovely breeze off the ocean and we share memories of the past year. Suddenly a Mariachi band appears. They smile broadly at us and surround our table.

Once again they sing *Ay, Ay, Ay, Ay* and we join in. This is great fun. As they finish, the leader stretches out his hand. Bob reaches into his jacket pocket where he carries all the cash and gives him a nice tip. Everyone is happy and they move on to the next table.

On the third day, we decide to visit the old Mayan ruins of Chiesa Nitsa. We board a rickety old bus, no air conditioning, for the four-hour journey. I take my favorite traveling companion, Dramamine. We open the windows wide and try to relax. I doze off and although sticky with sweat, feel quite rested. We walk along the path, which feels like a mile, lined with loud vendors hawking their wares. We finally arrive at the old ruins and are given a tour, learning about the Mayan practice of human sacrifice.

We see, in the distance, the two ziggurat-shaped, four-sided step pyramids, where the Mayans would carry the prisoners up to the top for sacrifice. The Castillo and Kukulkan Temples loom above, the latter 98 feet high. The tiny steps rise at a forty-five-degree angle. The kids start the climb. I realize how very small the Mayan people's feet were and I start to feel dizzy and nauseated.

"This is so cool, mom," says Jon.

"We can make it to the top," says Susan.

"Do you want to give it a try?" says Bob to me. He has size thirteen feet. How can he possibly climb those tiny steps? I am very reluctant but my family encourages me.

I walk up and up without looking back. The sun is a laser in my eyes, I am now sweating profusely. My family is at the top waving me on. When I reach the top I turn around and look down. I now know that I am going to die up here. I start to sway and the steps are an undulating blur. My husband notices how pale I look and tells me to sit down for a while on the top step. My children run up and down these teeny steps.

"Let me help you down," Bob says.

"No," I scream. "That will surely make me fall to my death. I have to do it alone."

I start the descent sideways, carefully placing one foot down at a time. I grip each step above with my hands. My legs have never been so tight. My fingers are stiff with fear. I am praying.

"Please God, help me."

By the time I reach the bottom my legs are shaking violently. I walk like Frankenstein for the rest of the day.

By the fourth day, we have adjusted to a comfortable routine. We love our days on the beach, the blue skies, the warm ocean water, the wonderful snorkeling, and the good food at the hotel. With two days to go, we decide to explore more of the island. We rent an available, 1970's vintage, dilapidated, Volkswagen Beetle.

The day is cool and windy so we wear jackets. We tour a beautiful national park with lush green foliage and colorful birds singing in the air. Next, we drive along the shoreline to see the natural beaches. Spectacular, soft, talc-like sand dunes, stretch for miles along the clear turquoise ocean.

"Dad let's stop here," shouts Susan.

"It's so amazing, just for a few minutes?" begs Jon.

It is afternoon and it has gotten quite warm so we leave our jackets in the car. As we step onto the beach we see a blue land crab scurry away. Before we know it the kids run along looking for treasure. Bob wades in the water and I sit on the sand enjoying the view.

We are reluctant to leave, but the sun is beginning to dip.

When we get to the car It becomes immediately apparent that something has changed.

"Oh my God, the cameras are gone!" I scream.

"Jesus Christ, Oh no!" yells Bob, grabbing his jacket from the back seat.

"All the money in my pocket is gone."

"Why didn't you lock the damn car?" I scream.

"It wouldn't lock!"

All our cash, except for the few dollars in our pants pockets has been stolen. We feel completely horrified and violated. How could we have been so foolish? We dejectedly ride back to town and decide to have an early dinner at a cafe with the few dollars we have left.

We sit at a table outside feeling angry and forlorn. We order enchiladas and Cokes and eat in silence. A Mariachi band appears out of nowhere. They surround our table with broad grins on their faces and begin to sing, *Ay, Ay, Ay, Ay*, with gusto. Their guitars and horns are in full swing.

This time we do not join in. We keep our heads down and eat silently. When they finish singing, the leader stretches out his hand for a tip.

"No money, nada," my husband laments with a shrug.

They don't seem to understand.

"You no like the music?" comes the reply.

"We like it but we have no money. It was all stolen."

He yells.

Suddenly their broad smiles turn into frowns. They press in closer around us.

One member taps me on the shoulder and says, "You have money, no?"

"Sorry, I don't."

Our family now leans forward, heads touching. We look at each other.

"What should we do?" Bob says.

The kids groan, "Oh no."

"This is scary!"

"Let's make a run for it," I say.

"Yes!" we all whisper.

Bob and I take the last dollars out of our pockets and slap them on the table.

"One, two, three, let's go." In one swift move, we push through the circle of musicians and make a wild run for the car. We pant and laugh hysterically when we reach the old VW.

We spend our last day and night at the hotel exhausted and resigned. The hotel clerk tells us there is no recourse for our losses. We are prime targets for the thieves on the island.

The clerk takes our credit card in payment and hopes we will return someday to the island of Cozumel.

I Do

Our beautiful daughter Susan is getting married.
Her black hair shines and her creamy skin glows. Her dark eyes sparkle with happiness.

She has been living in Brighton, Massachusetts with her boyfriend Elya for a year. Now he has proposed in a lovely way, on Mt. Chocorua, in the White Mountains of New Hampshire. They are marrying on August 13, 1994, at the historic mansion, Henderson House, in Weston, Mass.

We meet Elya on several occasions and find him handsome, loving and intelligent. They have not yet discovered all the flaws and frailties that one can only encounter in marriage.

Susan is in love.

Wedding plans are made. My husband Bob knows that his role is "Shut up, Show up, Pay up." He sweetly accepts this. Susan and I choose dresses, flowers, invitations, and food. We manage details with little conflict and actually have fun.

Ah, the wedding gown, all lace bodice, close-fitting, long sleeves, with just the right amount of cleavage, is perfect. The bridesmaids' dresses are a floral print on a black background.

We invite 130 people who all promise to come, some traveling great distances. Instead of the usual rehearsal dinner, there will be a party in a small Italian restaurant in the North End the night before the wedding. Elya and Susan rent it for the evening and invite everyone.

The party goes well. There is an open bar with lots of food. Everyone is having fun. We get to see friends and relatives alike. The old people cluster together in a cozy section of the restaurant eating appetizers and sipping wine.

At the bar, there is great hilarity, raucous laughter and lots of hugging among the young guests. They are doing "Shots." Vodka shots. This is new to me. Shots? How can they do that? That's what drunken barflies and Bowery bums do.

It is no longer my function to advise or comment. So, I say nothing. It has become clear that adult children hear suggestions as criticism, so how can I remark about my fears on the night before the wedding?

The old people leave the party around midnight. It is apparent that the party will go on without us. I remind Susan that I'll be picking her up at 10:00 a.m. the next morning for her beauty parlor appointment.

She agrees with a wonderful laugh.

In accordance with weather reports, the deluge begins at 3:00 a.m. It brings with it strong wind gusts, power outages, and torrential rain. The forecast tells us that It will not end until 4:00 p.m. on the wedding day. As arranged I get into my car at 9:45 a.m. in the blinding downpour to meet Susan at her apartment. I slosh out of the car into ankle-deep puddles. I ring the doorbell and wait forever.

She opens the door and I see the devastation. Her skin is pasty and green. Her long lovely hair is a bird's nest. Her eyes are puffy.

"Elya and I are very sick."

She moans.

"We didn't get home until 3 in the morning."

She begins to cry.

"Mom, I am so sorry. We drank too much."

We leave Elya in bed and drive through the drenching rain toward Salon Pini on Newberry Street. Halfway there we decide to stop at CVS for Alka Seltzer, bottles of water and Tums. Susan crushes an Alka Seltzer tab into a now half-empty bottle of water and drinks.

We drive through the streets of Boston in sheets of rain. Suddenly Susan screams, "Mom, pull over. Stop, NOW!!" I slam on the breaks, the car screeches into the curb. She opens the door just in time to vomit onto the street. Five cars pass by as she continues to vomit in the blinding rain.

Back in the car, Susan is a soaked puppy. She wraps herself in the blanket she finds on the back seat. She sips some water and chews a few Tums. We resume driving. They are waiting for us at Salon Pini and quickly lead Susan to the back.

I am free now to make phone calls. Most of the wedding guests are staying at the Marriott Hotel. I quickly find out there is no electricity there and none at Henderson House. No one can see to shave or take a shower. Neither is there air conditioning.

The food will be delivered, but with no refrigeration at Henderson House what will become of it?

The wedding is due to start at 5:00 p.m.

I am numb.

I check on Susan. The team at Salon Pini has dried her off and given her a cotton gown. They are working on her hair, each long strand being shaped into curls on top of her head. At the same time, they are doing her manicure and pedicure. She is hungry. I run to a nearby bagel shop in the rain. After she eats her color returns.

Everyone arrives at Henderson House on time. The lights magically go on and the air conditioning returns. The band begins to play. Everyone says, "Rain is good luck."

The rabbi is asking for two shots of scotch for his heart. *Again with the shots??* The music starts and the procession begins. Bob and I walk Susan down the aisle. Elya is a very pale green color and is swaying under the canopy.

I am still in a fog.

Finally, I hear my daughter say "I do." I hear Elya's loud "I do!" I hear the glass under his foot break. I see the bride and groom kiss. They are married.

I feel relief in knowing that everything has been taken care of and the celebration then takes on a life of its own. I am kissing and hugging guests, drinking wine and chatting with friends and relatives.

Karen, one of the bridesmaids, approaches me and says, "Marion, do you have a Benadryl?"

"No, why?"

Rachel, my son Jon's girlfriend, is having an allergy attack. She has eaten the chicken satay, *which has peanut sauce! Oh no!*

"Rachel is outside choking and vomiting. Jonathan called an ambulance."

"Oh God!"

I rush outside and see Annette, Bob's little sister who as predicted has become morbidly obese. She is smoking a cigarette. I ask if she has her mayonnaise-sized bottle of pills which she generally carries in her gargantuan purse.

"Yes, of course I do! Why?"

"You have a Benadryl?"

172

"Yes, I have anything you want. Why?"

She looks over and sees Rachel sitting on the curb coughing. Annette is concerned and reaches into her purse to remove the jar. With little effort, she finds a packet of Benadryl.

The ambulance pulls up. At the same time, Jon rushes up with a glass of water.

The EMT says, "We really can't do anything for her here. We have to take her to the hospital."

Rachel is swallowing two Benadryl's.

"I don't want to go to the hospital." We send the ambulance away and wait. Slowly the color returns to Rachel's face. She feels better.

We are finally back inside. Everyone is having fun eating, drinking, and dancing. The band is playing *Have Nagila.* Elya's ushers are lifting the bride and groom up on chairs. As they bounce up and down, I notice Elya's white knuckles clutching his chair. His pallid face is now blushing red as he leans over a bit too far.

With a broad grin, he suddenly regains composure.

Speeches are given. People laugh.
Susan and Elya are still in love.

I am pleased that they said, "I do!"

(R. to l.) Susan, Elya, Marion, Howard

Twins

"Hey, Mom, it's Jon."

"Hi Jon, what's going on?"

"All good stuff, Mom. Are you ready for this?"

"Sure, I love good stuff."

"Rachel and I are pregnant."

"Oh my God Jon, that's so great!"

"With twins, Mom."

"Jon, that's amazing. I am just thrilled for you both. I can't wait to tell dad!"

I'm thinking, Oy vey, how is that tiny little girl going to carry twins? Can they even begin to imagine how hard it will be to raise them? But I have learned to button my lips.

"Honey, just let us know how dad and I can help. We can hop on a plane at a moment's notice."

Jon and Rachel have been living in California for the last two years. He loves his work as a TV comedy writer and producer. I see no chance of them coming back east.

"Jon, is Rachel there? I'd love to congratulate her."

"To tell you the truth Mom, she's in the bathroom vomiting."

"Oh, I'm so sorry to hear that. But don't worry she'll probably stop feeling sick in three months."

I am thinking about my own pregnancies and deliveries with Jonathan and Susan. Such thrilling times. These will be our first grandchildren. I am hoping our daughter and son-in-law, Susan and Elya will be next. They are living in Boston, so much more accessible.

Months pass. Bob and I visit several times to watch the blooming, burgeoning belly grow. Rachel is feeling better. Love and excitement fill the air. By the sixth month, Rachel's back is swaying as she holds her hand on her hip. She has to sit down a lot.

"By the way," she says one day, "It's a boy and a girl."

"Wow, amazing!" I say.

"Incredible. Then you can close up shop," says Bob. Jon and Rachel roll their eyes.

"What!" says Bob. "You'll have a boy and a girl, who can ask for more?"

By month seven, Rachel is sitting and lying down a lot. When she stands, both hands are low on her back for balance. It is hard to digest food.

"We are going to have a C section sometime in April," says Jon.

"Great. That means we can plan to be there to see the delivery and to help out."

"Well," says Rachel, "my mother is coming the first two weeks, so we'll need you after that."

That's fine with me. I don't really want to see little Rachel being cut open or my son in scrubs, swaying dizzily. He'll be holding back his own regurgitation as he watches the bloody babies pulled out. Let her mother have that privilege. Any way do they allow grandparents in the delivery room?

"That will be perfect. I can stay as long as you need me."

At month eight Rachel is placed on bed rest. Bob and I spend the weekend with them to help around the house and bring her food. Her abdomen is a gigantic, bumpy monster. You can see the babies kicking and pressing an elbow here, a foot there.

"The doctor says Rachel has a great uterus," says Jon. "She can probably hold the twins to term." The baby girl now almost weighs six pounds and the boy five.

"Maybe they can deliver them a bit early," I say.

Oops! Exasperated looks and a bit of eye-rolling from the expectant parents.

"Mom, the docs know what they're doing."

I do not reply.

It is April 3rd and we leave for home the next day.

Back home, the phone rings. It is April 12th,1999

"Hey, Mom? It's Jon. Guess what, the babies were just born. They're both amazing, they're perfect. Rachel is fine. I watched the whole thing. I was in such a surreal zone that I didn't even feel queasy."

I cry and scream with joy.

"Bob, Bob, the babies are born and they are both great. Rachel is fine and Jon didn't even get sick."

"Gotta go Mom, talk soon."

"Love you, Jon."

"Love you, Mom."

"Wait, what are their names?" Too late. We find out later they are Ariel and Jakob.

On April 25th I am summoned to their three-level home on 5th street in Santa Monica. Rachel's mom caught a cold and has to leave. It is quite a nice contemporary house with a spiral staircase up to the loft where I will be sleeping. Below is the middle level with a living room and kitchen. Down another very narrow flight of stairs is the master bedroom and bath.

Rachel will be nursing both babies at the same time. It is the first time I have ever seen a nursing tire.

"What is that?' I ask.

"Isn't it cool?" says Rachel. "All the nursing moms have it." It is a spongy, soft flannel covered semi-circular pillow that the mom wears around her waist. The baby lays on it and is cradled comfortably to breastfeed. In this case, there are two babies suckling at the same time. Oh boy, quite a feat!

The babies need to nurse every hour and a half to two hours. These kids are VERY HUNGRY!!!

I have been given the night shift. The babies will be sleeping(?) in the living room. It is my job to stay alert. From my loft when I hear the twin's first cries, I am to run down the spiral staircase. Isn't it adorable how they begin to cry at the same time? I am then instructed to change the diapers, prepare a hot chocolate milk beverage for Rachel, and then carefully walk the babies, one in each arm, down the narrow stairs so that mommy can feed them.

Picture yourself in my situation. You realize that for two weeks you will not sleep. At all!

"I can do this," I say out loud.

For the first few nights of feedings I am exhilarated. The babies cry, I go down the spiral stairs to warm the milk for Rachel, then change each diaper. The babies scream with hunger. Once changed I maneuver them down the narrow stairs together. I put one baby over my left shoulder. I bend down, and one-handedly, slide my free hand under baby number two. I throw the baby over the waiting shoulder. Oh God this kid could go flying across the room. Now, how to bring down the drink? I take two trips. I gingerly walk down the narrow flight of steps and hand the screaming babies to Rachel.

"Thanks Marion, do you have my drink?"

"I'll go right up and get it dear."

This happens four times every night.

One night I forget to wash my hands after handling poopy diapers and get an eye infection. I go to a local doctor for eye drops. I take the shopping list with me. I had hoped to catch up on sleep during the day. This is not to be.

I think back to the time I was nursing Jonathan. He was never satiated so the pediatrician told me to give him a supplemental bottle after each feeding.

"Don't worry," the doctor had said, "The baby will always go back to the breast."

Suddenly, a light bulb!

One day after a week has passed, very tired, I say, "Rachel, what do you think of the idea of giving each of the twins a supplemental bottle after each breastfeeding? They are so hungry, they might sleep longer. If you like I'd be happy to do that. You'd get more sleep as well."

"Oh, I don't know, I really want to only breastfeed them. Everyone says that is the healthiest thing to do."

"I certainly understand and basically agree with your thinking on that." Enough said. We continue the regimen.

A day later Jon approaches me in the kitchen.

"Mom, got a minute?"

"Sure, what's up?"

"Rachel is wondering if you can show more respect for her way of feeding the babies."

My face feels as if it's burning red. Tears fill my eyes and I turn away. I try to maintain a calm demeanor.

"Of course, I respect her method. I only thought it would be helpful." I turn to the stove to boil a kettle of water.

"Thanks Mom, you have really been a wonderful help to us. We couldn't have done it without you."

I do not reply.

At the end of my two-week detention I, too, catch a cold and go home. There are lots of thank you's and hugs all around. They have hired a woman to come in every day to help.

Jon will take the night shift.

Jacob and Ariel

Fiftieth Wedding Anniversary

It always amazes me when family vacations actually turn out well.

Our children and grandchildren live in California so getting together is no easy task. It is even more difficult to plan reunions that are really fun and stress-free. This time Bob and I try hard to arrange a vacation to celebrate our 50th wedding anniversary hoping it might work for everyone.

We decide on Hawaii because it is easier for the kids to get there. We, the martyrs, say we don't mind the eleven-hour flight going, the flights from Island to Island and the three flights back, including the red-eye.

Bob and I start off alone on the island of Kauai, a most beautiful paradise. Poi Pu beach, where our hotel is located, is famous for its snorkeling, Bob taking full advantage. I hear, "Don't touch that turtle, they snap!"

The warm weather, the wonderful, calm green water, and soft sand are all perfect for healing his brand new knees. When we return, I say to him, "I told you to use sunscreen!"

A later helicopter ride around the island offers spectacular views never to be seen on land.

Our next stop, Maui, again makes us happy with amazing seafood to eat and magnificent fish to see, swimming near the surface of coral reefs. Back in the hotel, I tell Bob, "I feel so nauseated. Do you think it's the raw shrimp?"

Finally the treat we have been waiting for. We meet up with the family on the Big Island. We are twelve, our children Jon and Sue, their spouses, and six grandchildren. We choose the Hilton Waikoloa because it is kid-friendly. The kids love the sparkling lagoon with easy snorkeling, kayaking, water surfing and swims with dolphins.

Thanksgiving dinner at the Waikoloa is all I could wish for. We sit at a round table for twelve. How do they manage to get Thanksgiving dinner so delicious? Juicy turkey, crunchy stuffing, glistening candied sweets, creamy white potatoes and gravy, succulent pumpkin and apple crumb pies. No cooking for me, no preparation, no cleanup. This is so good.

So what are we all thankful for? I am so thankful for playing a part in the creation of this amazing family.

Five-year-old Gabriel speaks out.

"You created us? What? What does that mean mom?"

Giggling all around.

"I'll tell you later, dear," replies Susan.

Bob is grateful for having the family together for our fiftieth anniversary.

Next son Jon and daughter Susan raise their glasses and tell us how important we have been in their lives, how wonderfully we connect (except when we don't). They know we are always there for them and their families. They take the opportunity to include their spouses, without whom none of the children would exist either.

More giggles.

Everyone then joins in:
"Happy Anniversary Mom and Dad."

"Thanks for this trip Grandma and Grandpa."
"Where can we go next year?"
"We love you Grandma and Grandpa."

"We love you too."

And so it goes.

Joey, Jon, and Bob

The Flight

On an airplane, I never breathe a final sigh of relief until we are safely on the ground in New Jersey. I consider my deep breathing—deep breath, hold it in, let it out slowly—to be a lucky charm that usually works. Along with Bonine, it tends to work well. Not so much this time.

We are to take three flights home from our family vacation in Hawaii. First from the big island to Honolulu, second from Honolulu to LA. The final flight is the red-eye from LA to Newark. By the third leg we are ready to get some sleep.

Bob and I sit across the aisle from each other, he settles in at his window. I love the aisle seat so I can easily get up and out to the bathroom.

As I approach my seat I see a young woman at the window and a dog relaxing on the middle seat.

"Oh, what's this?" I think. Before I say more than "Hi" the young woman speaks up.

"This is my service dog, Henry, I'm hoping that no one shows up for the middle seat so he can have it."

"Ok," I answer. "What kind of dog is he?"

"He's a Pomeranian Chihuahua."

"How cute."

Henry looks up at me with big, brown, intelligent eyes. As I slip into my seat, I begin to pet him. He is licking my hand all over. I think, "Short hair, no allergy problem here."

Before long, three, very loud, large, obviously Russian people enter the plane, the kind of people you hope will pass you by. But no. They stop right at our row, carrying large bags of luggage. They are a husband, a wife, and a teenage daughter. The husband has a massively huge stomach and grunts as he tries desperately to squeeze his soft leather suitcase into the compartment above me.

HE IS MY MIDDLE SEAT GUY!

A flight attendant shows up and says, "Excuse me. You'll have to empty some of the items from that bag so it can fit."

"Vot the hell?" He grumbles.

He is leaning on me as he presses thermal wear, a sweater, and trousers into a space in the compartment, cursing under his breath. The wife and daughter, speaking in rapid Russian, clamor into the two seats next to Bob and put a large tan case, with what looks like air holes, under the seat. Do I hear a yipping sound? Now the puppy next to me is whimpering and shaking violently at the approach of this big Russian bear of a man. The young woman comforts Henry as she puts him in his case and under the seat.

Without hesitation, this gigantic man, now shiny with sweat says to me, "Vill you change seats vit me so I can have de aisle?"

"I'm so sorry, but no," I say. "I need the aisle to get to the bathroom."

As he wriggles and thrusts himself past me, he spits his words for all to hear.

"Some people do not know how to co-operate! Some people have no manners!"

I wipe the spray from my forehead and look away.

What do you do at a moment like this?

I am painfully aware that I will have to spend the next five hours sitting next to this man, who has now begun to emit a pungent, cabbagey odor. I say nothing. We are about to take off. We, all three, have our hands on our knees hoping to avoid the possibility of touch. Fat man in the middle can not help but spread his body out on all sides, grazing my left knee. I Think being nice might help. I offer him a piece of gum.

"No!" he growls.

"Ok."

The cabin lights go out, "Let's try to sleep."

Sleep never comes to me, but the girl at the airplane window has curled up and is quietly snoring. Big man next to me sleeps hard, wheezing every fifth breath until he has to go to the bathroom and pushes his body over me without a word. On his return, he approaches his wife.

"Where is the zoup you brought. Give it here."

The wife obeys, giving him a thermos. He shoves past me and opens the thermos. This is a smell I am not familiar with. It's a garlicky, sausagy and cabbagy odor. Perhaps a note of beet. Fat man pours it into the cup and begins to slurp. I feel nauseated.

My deep breathing escalates. I am breathing so deeply that my fingertips are tingling.

I am hyperventilating.

At the same time my hand that was licked all over by the tiny dog, Henry, has begun to feel itchy. Pretty soon I feel itchy all over and shuffle through my purse for my Benadryl. Apparently, even short-haired dogs don't agree with me. I take the pill and try to calm myself with pleasant thoughts of food recipes.

I wait for our arrival.

The captain warns of turbulent weather over the Rocky Mountains. I brace myself and pray. Here come the bumps. I grip my folded arms and clench my teeth. I breathe even more deeply. Husband Bob remains in the arms of the dream god Morpheus at his window seat.

When we finally hit the ground safely I am thankful.

Suddenly I hear the yipping sound coming from under the seat of the Russian wife. She pulls up the case and opens it. It is another Chihuahua. It looks like a yellow rat. She pets it lovingly and talks to it soothingly in Russian.

Fat man shoves past me before we get permission to stand. He rummages overhead to put his stuff back in his bag. He presses his body parts against my arm.

Do I smell a touch of urine mixed with cabbage?

Please let me die.

Who's That Rapping at my Door?

A faint smell of fresh paint lingers in the air. My daughter-in-law Rachel has opened all the windows to air out my weekend apartment in the Pacific Palisades. Everything is white. The living room has a white linen sofa and white throw pillows. Oddly one pillow is red. Two white club chairs. A glass table sits on a fluffy white rug. A large flat-screen TV is on the white wall.

The kitchen has white appliances, cabinets, and countertops, all apparently new. The bathroom is tiled white with a white sink. Even the towels are white. My favorite is the bedroom. The sleigh bed is covered completely in white– sheets, pillows and comforter. A few white, lacy scatter pillows. Strangely again there sit two red throw pillows. Nothing more.

The wood floors shine. There is color in the framed impressionist paintings and museum prints, some of my favorites. One of Van Gogh's sailboats reminds me of the series that hung in my parent's bedroom.

The apartment is in a large white stucco house. Apparently, the house is divided into three apartments. One is across the hall. The other is directly above me. There are several brick steps at the entrance, lined on both sides with flowering plants. I will be staying here for three nights.

I have fallen in love with the apartment. I love its proximity to town and my children's house, the farm market, and Starbucks. I can walk everywhere.

I am here to see my three grandchildren in the musical of Alice in Wonderland at Theater Palisades. I will get to hang out with the family and see all three performances. Rachel's mom Susanne is visiting as well.

"Renee, I'm here in town. I'm just confirming our lunch date. My cousin Donna is joining us too."

"Marion, that's great. I made the reservation at Maison Gerard. It's on Swathmore, right? I can't wait to see the kids in *Alice!*"

"Perfect. I'll walk over and meet you both at the restaurant. I'm so excited to see you!" Nothing like old college friends.

Each performance is better than the next. I love sitting in the theater with my son Jon, Rachel, Renee and Donna. The show is hilarious and so professional. Ariel is the doorknob, a butterfly and one of the cards. Joey is the king and Jakob is the mad hatter–perfect casting. The kids are adorable. I am taken too with the boisterous and hilarious Red Queen.

"Off with her head!! Off with their heads!" Her famous lines!

We all hang out at dinner and watch the opening night of the London Olympics on tv.

"Mom, you must be exhausted. It's 1:00 a.m. back east. I'll drive you to your apartment."

"You're so right Jon, I need sleep."

Jon drives me to the apartment and sees me inside.

When he leaves I deadbolt the door and prepare to sleep. I'm tired but wonder if I can rest after such an exciting day. I climb up into the wonderful bed. I wait, covering up under the fluffy comforter.

But what is that sound? A gentle scratching? A mouse? Do I hear a slight tapping?

I'm aware of footsteps from the apartment above. The marching becomes louder, a kind of heavy pacing back and forth. Then a gentle rapping. On the wall? Is it my imagination? I am reminded of Edgar Allen Poe's, *The Raven*.

While I nodded nearly napping, suddenly there came a tapping, as of someone gently rapping, rapping at my chamber door. Tis some visitor, I muttered, tapping at my chamber door...only this and nothing more.

I am terrified but talk myself down.

Covering my head, I snuggle under the comforter and finally fall into a fitful sleep.

Bright and early, a bit groggy, I am ready to get out of the apartment for my walk to Starbucks. I open the door and nearly bump into a young woman who is about to walk down the stairs. She wears heavy hiking boots.

"Hi, I'm your upstairs neighbor. Beautiful day!"

"Hi, yes it is."

She scampers off ahead of me. I watch her long blond ponytail swing as she bounces down the street.

My morning is filled with lovely events. Brunch with friends and shopping. Best of all I make several purchases at the farmers market. I don't mention last night's experience.

I love cooking with the kids so I buy two perfect eggplants, five zucchini's, two fresh tomatoes, a dozen eggs and a block of cheddar cheese for the evening dinner. We will make cheese souffle and ratatouille.

After another great performance, it's back to the house to cook with the children.

"Ratatouille? What's that?" laughs Jakob

"Yeah, Ratatouille? Is that the rat from the animated movie?" They love saying the word and giggle.

"We don't want to eat a rat," jokes Ariel.

"I still think grandma is going to make us eat a rat!" Joey quips. They google *ratatouille* and realize it's an eggplant, tomato, and zucchini dish.

"Oh, it sounds good!" says Ariel.

"Well, sort of good," says Jakob skeptically.

We beat, cut and bake. The children learn about a roux that is needed for the souffle. They learn how to separate the eggs and fold in the beaten egg whites into the cheesy roux. They are great students. We have so much fun. Everyone loves the fluffy souffle.

Susanne and I like the ratatouille. The kids taste it skeptically.

"I like it," says Joey."

"I sort of like it," says Jakob.

"I love it!" says Ariel.

"Nice," says Jon.

I'm a bit nervous when Jon takes me back to the apartment. I haven't mentioned last night's experience. Maybe it was a dream? This is my last night. I wish that my husband Bob was with me. I'm never frightened with him around.

"Goodnight Mom. It was a great day."

"Goodnight Jon. I am so happy to be here."

"Love you."

"Love you."

I deadbolt the door. I prepare for bed and listen for noises. I brush my teeth. Is that a faint tapping on the bathroom window?

I think I'd better take a sleeping pill.

I climb under the comforter and wait. There it is again, the heavy pacing. It seems like a tormented soul obsessively stomping across the floor. Now I hear a gentle tapping on the window.

Oh God, I'm terrified.

I hunker under the covers and pray. The sleeping pill begins to take hold. In my troubled dream I see the two red pillows turn into Red Queens. They shout in my face. Their mouths are open, black holes.

"Off with her head! Off with her head!!"

At 6:00 a.m. I am more than ready to leave the apartment. I dress quickly. Suddenly there's a gentle tapping at the door. Is this for real? The tapping is now a rapping, then a knocking. I shake with fright.

I approach the door but refuse to open it.

"Who is it?" I scream, too loudly.

"It's your upstairs neighbor!"

"What do you want?" I shout.

"I just wanted to say Hi!"

"Well Hi! But I'm not going to open the door!"

"That's okay. See you later. Bye."

I wait to hear her hiking boots on the stairs. I look out the window and watch the young woman walk toward town.

Her long blond ponytail swings in the breeze.

I feel a shudder pass through me.

I Saw Grandma Naked

My excitement mounts as I approach the house on the corner. As I tiptoe down the maze of the pathway I begin to feel the love.

The doorbell is broken, so no response. My knocks are futile. I open the door and step into a house where I always feel welcome. It is the home of my son Jon, his wife Rachel and their sweet family.

I remember the chaos of my own life when the children were little. This house is a living, breathing organism. It represents the love and toil of a mommy, daddy, and three young children.

I push past piles of shoes and laundry in the hallway to reach the living room. A love seat, two comfortable chairs, and a coffee table beckon to me. They are piled high with layers of newspapers, magazines, children's books, mail, plastic toys, and sippy cups. This archeological dig is inviting me to stay.

When I clear a path to the kitchen I see the remains of yesterday's nourishing meals. Cereal dishes, unfinished sandwiches, cups of milk, yogurt containers and last night's Chinese takeout. The kitchen table is a mountain of play toys and art materials.

"Hello, anybody home? Where are you?"

Coming from the outdoor atrium I hear voices, then screaming. I peek out to see my three adorable grandchildren, Ariel, Jakob, and Joey. The twins are six and Joey is three.

"Mommy, Mommy, Jakob just squished his mud muffin in my hair."

Ariel screams.

I'm looking around for mommy.

The children are making mud pies and muffins.

These kids are very creative. They use watercolors and finger paints. Their artwork is displayed all over, not only on the refrigerator but on the walls. Today they are pretending to bake.

"Mommy, Mommy, she did it to me first."

But where is mommy? I look around.

The phone is ringing, but I can't find it.

The little ones run into the house.

"Hi, Grandma!" They all yell.

190

They run toward me with muddy fingers. I kneel down and they hug my face and squeeze my hands.

"Come and see what we've made. It's for you."

They take my hands and lead me to their garden in the enclosed back yard. They have planted sweet potatoes, peas and avocado pits to see what will grow. Mostly they love playing in the dirt. Mom usually supplies water for the mud muffins and cakes.

I have heard that children who are too clean get sick more often. Playing with mud has to be healthy. I control my desire to go back in to wash my hands and face. The fighting begins again. Mud flies back and forth. Everyone cries and laughs.

Suddenly, like magic, Mommy appears.

She and I quickly hug and both laugh at the situation.

"Ok, guys, that's enough. Upstairs you go for your baths."

They follow each other up the stairs like little ducklings. I am very impressed. She is the best mommy ever!

When my husband and I visit we are relegated to the office-guestroom-playroom-jumping-off-the-futon room. We scrounge for towels and sheets in the "clean" laundry basket and make do with the downstairs bathroom at the end of the hall. It has a door that doesn't lock. The shower is encased in smoky glass. The water takes twenty minutes to get warm.

This time I am visiting alone. I will endure anything to spend time with these adorable, lovable children. I love their sticky hugs and wet kisses, the messy clothing and disheveled hair. I love the games we play and love sitting on the very well-worn family room couch reading stories.

On this visit, one morning, I awake early. As usual, I try to hop into the shower before the family rises. Have I mentioned that I am very fastidious, a germaphobe? Did I mention that I love my privacy?

This morning the children are all awake. They are down the hall in the family room, quietly watching TV and drinking their warmed chocolate milk.

I slither along the wall and tiptoe into the bathroom. I turn on the shower and lay out my towel and clothing on the toilet seat. I wait for the water to get hot. I undress and finally slip into the shower knowing that the water will turn cold after five minutes, tops. I lather up all over and begin to enjoy the warm water beating down on me.

Suddenly there's a knock on the door!

" I have to go!" the voice screams. It's little Joey

"I can't wait!"

And then, bang, bang, push, push, the door flings open. There stands little Joey looking directly at me through the smoked glass. I scream in horror and place soapy hands on my private areas as best I can. Joey giggles as he tosses my things to the floor, urinates in the toilet, and runs out, leaving the door wide open.

"I just saw Grandma naked!" he screeches.

"Come and see, come and see!"

I quickly turn off the water and reach my hand out for the towel. They are all back in a flash, but all they see now is a very wet and soapy grandma holding up a towel.

"I see her too, I see her too!" the others yell.

I am in control when I calmly say, "Kids, get out of here."

"No Grandma, we can see you naked!" They laugh hysterically.

I am no longer calm.

"Get out of here! Get the hell out of here right now!" I yell uncontrollably.

"Ooh, noo, grandma just cursed, Grandma is cursing." They are doubling over with raucous laughter.

"Oooh, Grandma you're cursing!"

With one hand I push them out just as the towel drops. I slam the door shut. I shake with anxiety and humiliation.

I can't help but laugh.

I will be back!

L to r: Joey, Ariel, and Jakob

Travel

I have found that there ain't no surer way to find out if you like people or hate them than to travel with them. — Mark Twain

The real voyage of discovery consists not in seeking new landscapes but in having new eyes. — Marcel Proust

Hermaphrodite

Hermaphrodite: *One having the sex organs and many of the secondary sex characteristics of both male and female.*

It is with great delight that my college roommate Marge and her husband Dave love our company. I don't know why. It is unusual for four people to get along so well for so long. They visit us everywhere we live and join us on every vacation. Family sojourns surprise us when their children, Mark and Nancy get along famously with our kids. Amazing? Yes.

No experience stands out as vividly as our trip to Italy in 1997.

We are lucky to rent a typical villa in Camaiore, Tuscany. It's the very place where the famous sculptor named Fiore de Henriques, lives atop the mountain, Per Alta. She is a hermaphrodite. We are told that she is sometimes happy to invite guests to her castle fortress on the hill.

We call to ask if she will receive us. I speak to her secretary, Elizabeth and discover that we are welcome to come up and meet with her.

After a hearty breakfast of tomato and cheese frittatas and crusty bread, along with morning mimosa's we are ready to embark on this journey. I must tell you that here in Tuscany we are in love with the delicious food and superb wines. A meal does not go by when we do not imbibe with gusto.

Well-fortified and high on more than life, we chug up up up in our little rented Fiat, on a road of hairpin turns, to Per Alta. The car strains to its limit. Suddenly we reach the pinnacle. We see the large stone, mildly dilapidated, mansion. It sits among mature olive and lemon trees, heavy with fruit.

As we pull up to the portico and step from the car, a tall magnificent person emerges from the house with open arms. The feathered, shoulder-length, silver hair, parted in the middle, is regal. The broad shoulders and straight back imply a strong masculine quality. This individual smiles broadly. One cannot truly say whether it is a man or a woman. Fiore wears a loosely belted smock over knee-breeches and tall, soft suede boots all in the Cossack style.

She obviously has breasts. But the six-foot height and wide shoulders speak of a masculine countenance. Over the smock, around her shoulders, she wears a magnificent, long, curly sheepskin lined vest. Her arms spread wide as she engulfs us in hugs. Her dark sparkling eyes look deeply into each of our faces as she shakes our hands.

"Welcome, Benvenuto." In a deep, jovial voice Fiore introduces us to Elizabeth, her sweet-natured British secretary.

"Come in, come in!"

She immediately herds us into a large wood-paneled and glass-enclosed room which looks out across the valley to the sea and a distant outline of Corsica. Her sculptures are everywhere, several of famous people. Sculptures of twins, doubles, siblings and pairs, a repeated motif in stone and bronze are found inside and out. They dot Per Alta's narrow pathways and steps.

A young man named Anton appears carrying a tray with glasses of red wine, cheeses, and crackers. Fiore invites us to sit on the stone patio, looking down to the valley. It is a clear sunny day and our host is most talkative.

"That's the Lipschitz house down there. And look you can see the Mediterranean and the tip of Corsica."

She is referring to her good friend the famous sculptor.

Without hesitation she tells us of her life, her upbringing in Trieste, and her harrowing experiences with Mussolini's dictatorship. She tells us how she came to be a sculptor and most of all about her family. The young man, our waiter, keeps refilling our wine glasses. The deep purple wine is thick and richly delicious.

Our beautiful host confides the love she had for her brother, how she adored her father, but how she hated her mother.

"My mother used to call me a monster. But I didn't feel like a monster, a third sex, yes, but I was quite honored. I felt part of the Greek legends."

Marge and Dave show interest in her work and talk about buying one of her pieces. They are laughing and joking together.

Dave turns to his wife and says for all to hear, "I really love his work!"

An angry look darkens Fiore's handsome face.

She grabs her breasts with both hands, "Do not be mistaken, I am a woman!" she yells.

We are taken aback. David apologizes and gulps his wine. Everyone quiets. The waiter quickly appears, this time with a tray of artichokes, marinated mushrooms, and olives, chocolates, and cigars. The wine is a sweet and spicy Amaro. He serves it in tiny cut glass cordial glasses.

"Oh, no, what now?"

Undaunted Bob and Dave and our host take up the gigantic cigars as the waiter, Anton, uses a flaming lighter to ignite each one.

Comrades again. The moment is saved.

It is getting late and the sun has begun to dip. Our jovial host invites us to come back tomorrow for lunch. We are thrilled. Tipsy, we stagger to the Fiat. David is driving and speeding around the paper clip turns. I am in the back seat feeling dizzy and nauseated, praying for God's help.

The next morning we awake to another sparkling, sunny day. We share croissants and cheese omelets along with spicy Bloody Mary's. We are promising to keep our vodka consumption to a minimum. We are giggling with anticipation. It is time to embark, one more time, up the steep mountain to Per Alta.

"Don't forget the cameras!"

"Let's get some more shots of her work!"

"I want a picture of the Lipschitz house down in the valley."

This time, with Bob driving, we slowly wind our way up the treacherous mountain. I notice that, to our left, there is a rocky cliff going straight down with no guardrail. I turn away, feeling dizzy.

We are greeted effusively again by our host Fiore. Elizabeth ushers us to our seats around a very large wooden table where we find other invited guests. There is the house painter from Brooklyn who is doing work on the estate. Also a handsome and funny gay, guy couple who are old friends of Fiore. Two young women artists visiting from the States grin and shake our hands with vigor, as we all sit.

The meal is simple and delicious. Crunchy, brick-baked chicken with rosemary, escarole salad, spinach cooked in olive oil and grilled potatoes. Loaves of crusty bread with olive oil to dip, along with free-flowing, delicious red and white wines. Our glasses are never empty. The luscious Italian grapes are the elixir of life.

Fiore sits at the head of the table. She has everyone introduce themselves and asks us to tell a little about ourselves. We are a very compatible group, and find ourselves joking and laughing together, telling how we each came to meet our host and complimenting her at every opportunity.

We love her work. We love her.

We linger at lunch for three hours. It is now 4:00 p.m. and the sky has darkened. It has begun to rain. Still jocular and drunk we decide it is time to leave. Dave insists on driving, saying that he is, by far, the best driver in our group. We kiss and hug our host and new friends with a promise to return next year. We strap ourselves into our little car with the men sitting in front.

Now it is raining hard.

Slowly, slowly we head down the twisted road. We are more than halfway down when we start to slide forward. David has difficulty controlling the car. His foot is on the brake but we continue to slip. He brings us to a sharp stop and pulls up the emergency brake. I sit behind him and look out to see that the back right wheel is hanging out over the cliff. I am, at once, terrified, dizzy and nauseated.

We all scream.

"Oh, God, what should we do?"

"We're going to die!"

Our drunk and fearless driver yells a command.

"You guys get out and start walking down the hill!"

How can we leave him alone to navigate this disaster?

"I can do this, but I need to do it myself."

After yelling and crying, we get out and leave him to it. Three of us find an inlet in the mountain several feet away.

We pray out loud.

"Help him, God."

"We have children, God!"

Slowly David puts the stick shift into first gear.

Slowly, with one foot on the clutch and the other on the accelerator, he eases the emergency brake down. We see the car lurch forward as he straightens the wheel.

"He did it!" we scream. We clap and jump up and down.

Shaking, we get into the car and slowly complete the journey.

We shriek and laugh all the way down.

David yells, "I never could have done that sober!"

White Water

If I pretend to be sick maybe I won't have to go. It's 3:00 a.m., there's no way I can get any sleep. This white water thing is scaring me too much. I need a plan, a plan. I need to plot a way to stay here in San Jose. Oh no, it's an overnight trip. I'm doomed. I have to do this! Oiii, Oyyyy.

The Pacuare River in Costa Rica is said to be one of the most beautiful and ecologically friendly rivers in the world. It runs for eighty miles to the Caribbean and is a top river for white water rafting. Its rapids are rated from III to IV. The river is surrounded by untouched rain forest and is home to various species of birds, jaguars, monkeys, and ocelots.

Bob and I awake at 6:00 a.m. in time to meet our rafting party at the beach, including friends David and his wife Marge. I sit at breakfast in groggy silence. I don't want to appear afraid, but it's impossible for me to eat anything or smile. We are driven to the beach where we will be prepped for the journey down the river. We'll be traveling for two days on one of six rafts.

It is immediately obvious that we four are the oldest adventurers in the group. The other travelers are probably in their thirties and forties. They wear spandex and speedos. Both men and women are "ripped," or are they *buff?* Everyone's wearing tank tops, their tan muscles bulging. They all turn to look at us in our cotton tee-shirts and baggy Bermudas. Are they giggling and pointing at us? Or is it my imagination?

We know that there will be instructions of some kind before we travel down the river to our death. Our guides, stocky and strong, young native men, are in a huddle. They are a group of six, one for each rubber death trap. One stands out from the rest. He is very tall and has broad shoulders. The leader? They also seem to be looking over at us, checking us out and whispering.

We awkwardly await our doom.

I imagine the tall guy saying, "I'll take them."

Finally, the tall leader comes over to us. He smiles broadly.

"Hi, my name is Andre. You will join me in the lead raft. Don't worry I'll take good care of you. All you have to do is follow my instructions and you will have an amazing time."

We nod agreement and shake hands all around. Does he notice that my palms are cold and clammy?

"Andre, I have to tell you something."

"What is it Marion?" *Wow, he remembers my name!*

"Well Andre, I have never done this before and I am scared to death!"

"Well Marion, don't you worry, I have never done this before either!! That makes two of us!!"

Ha, Ha! Marge and I titter nervously. Bob and David guffaw too loudly. I know he's kidding, right?

"You are to wear your helmets at all times. You will sit on the edges of the raft. When I yell paddle, you paddle hard. Try to keep the rhythm. The river is rough today so the rapids are about a four, maybe five."

Did he say four maybe five? That's as rough as it gets! My heart pounds in my throat.

"Okay, let's go."

We gingerly step into the raft, each sitting on the edge, feet inside. We are given our paddles and we push off. The Pacuare River is calm and green. The sun shines and we can see the lush jungle all around us. A gentle breeze cools our faces.

"When we hit the white water I will tell you to throw yourselves and your paddles down into the raft. I'll take over!"

I expect the worst.

Nevertheless, I begin to relax. We are all paddling in perfect synch. This is lovely.

The water gets rougher and I can see what looks like a waterfall ahead.

The raft speeds up and spins around. I hang on to keep from falling out. Andre straightens the raft as we speed towards the rapids.

Andre yells, "Get down! Get down now!"

Marge and I throw ourselves and our paddles to the bottom of the raft. Bob and Dave are trying to act brave and keep paddling. Andre yells again

"Get down!"

So they do. I feel the bumping and gushing of the raft against the white water. We are pummeled from side to side. We scream in terror.

When it is over we look up to see Andre laughing. We emerge from the bottom soaking wet.

"You did great guys. Up you go. Back to paddling."

The river is once again serene as we paddle with the current. We are lulled into a state of calm as the sun bakes down.

Every now and then Andre calls out, "Take a break." We put our paddles on our laps and drift along. We see the other rafts in the distance behind us.

I feel a slight inkling of pride. I did it, and I'm alive.

At least so far!

POEMS

Poetry lifts the veil
  from the hidden beauty
  of the world
And makes familiar objects be
  as if they were not familiar
—*Percy Shelley*

Poetry:
It's that time of night, lying in bed,
thinking what you really think,
Making the private world public
That's what poetry does
—*Allen Ginsberg*

Unicorn and the Zebra

Grandma you are a Unicorn
You have magical powers
Can you heal my wounded heart?

Ariel, no, I am a Zebra
I am black and white
I follow the herd

But grandma you are wise
Independent, mysterious too
I want to be like you

Ariel, no, I am a Zebra
I need community
You have beauty and strength
You are a Unicorn

Grandma, Zebras are wild
and free
Not just black and white
No fears, they are Strong

Ariel, there is the paradox
I can only sleep surrounded by the herd
You are free to roam
You will heal your heart

Grandma, is the world black or white?
Is it happy or sad? Strong or weak?
A gray whirling mass?
Something in between?

Ariel, yes, there is a middle ground
Take the risk
Find your own path
You are a Unicorn

Porto Wine

Perpetual blue sky, hot sun warms my face
We climb to lush green terraces of vineyards
where grapes are bruised and crushed
into
Purple wine

Far below the Conversos warmed by the same sun
walked the streets of old city, Porto
Bruised and crushed by the Inquisition
to a
bloody death

Hairpin turns to Sandeman winery
Our tongues taste dark sweet liquid.
We roar with joyous laughter
at its
warmth

Down below Conversos refusing to obey a king
who punishes them, taking their farms and cattle
With orders from the Pope to rid the land
tongues tasting the bitter bile of despair

Purple grapes pressed and tortured into
Sweet, Tangy port
Luscious seafood, a sumptuous buffet
Tourists high on life
and wine

Conversos pressed and tortured
Confess a secret observance
Families fearing for life must run

Or die

Who Will it Be?

The Reaper is looking grim today
searching for his likely prey
No one knows who's going next
How clever

He slithers and slides from
town to town
Without a sound, he slips
under a door

His scythe is in the closet
a tender touch will do
He takes his time
Who will it be?

I feel him whisper in my ear,
his silent breath burns hot
Then turns to ice
When will he come for me?

The Reaper is looking grim today
searching for his likely prey
He alone knows who's next to go
How clever

Velma, Checkout Lady

How long have you worked
here?
A long time, A long time

I always choose your line,
I like your line
I've known you a long time,
a long time

I'm here thirty-one years,
thirty-one years
I remember you too

I always choose your line
You are quick and friendly,
quick and friendly
I always choose your line

I like the food you buy
Healthy things like yogurt
and fruit
And broccoli

I remember when she was
young. The face puffy now
The large brown eyes
baggy, the stomach fat.
She was pretty once.

I always choose your line
You are quick and friendly,
quick and friendly
I always choose your line

I remember your kids, she
says, they were funny and
cute
They are all grown up now
I never had kids, she says

So many years ago, will
you retire soon?
The pension not so good
for part-time. I have to stay
I like it here. It's my family

I'll see you next time then

Thanks for bagging
Thank you for bagging

Thank you for everything
Bye now

Goodbye

Walking

I walk from where I have gone
I walk to where I am going
I walk away from the past
I walk into the future
My pace is erratic

You have Haglund's Deformity
the doctor says
What is that?
It's that bump on your heel
Will I be able to walk?
Stretch and Ice, Stretch and Ice

Life, a long walk
Life, a conversation
Every step faces both ways
An ending.
A beginning

You have Achilles Tendinitis
the doctor says
What is that?
It's the tightness in your heel
It really hurts
Stretch and Ice, Stretch and Ice

The pathways I walk are pathways I live
The trail leads forward to new destinations
Walking and talking along the way
To those I love
and to those who are indifferent

It will get better
the doctor says
When will it get better?
It takes a long time

I Don't Have A Long Time

Nantucket View
Arrogance of Seagulls

A seagull with Vladimir Putin eyes
slightly crossed, struts by
looking for prey

Proud head bobbing from side to side
eying our blanket
Steely, stealthy diligence, he takes his time

With pointy laser beak he steps boldly
over the line
to attack the chips

Everyone curses and screams
at his arrogance and power
But he is gone

Anthony Bourdain
Parts Unknown

B. June 25, 1956, D. June 8, 2018
New York Times: *Anthony Bourdain's body was free of narcot-*
ics at the time of death.

Your craggy profile is a
delicate sculpture
Your gray hair curls, your lips smile
But your eyes are sad

Graceful and tall, tattoos firm
on the muscle
Celebrity Chef, clever adventurer
everyone loves Anthony Bourdain
But your eyes are sad

You eat Octopus and snake,
reindeer and yak
with gusto
You drink Bourbon and beer, whatever
is offered. "I could drink a lot of these."
But your eyes are sad

You kicked your heroin habit, you're healthy
it seems
Bhutan is the end of the road
interviews go well
With hearty laughter
you eat two hard-boiled eggs
But your eyes are sad

You walk the path to your room
And hang yourself with your belt

Swan Song

The Swan glides silently for all her life
never making a sound
except for an occasional honk

My life's one loud off-kilter song.
With rhythmic uncertain beat I dance
thrashing along noisily fighting the inevitable

Just before death, in a final gesture
the swan gives a loud
musical performance
One fearful, long, bleating, song

My swan song is a slow wearisome joke
a swaying acceptance of what's to come
If I am lucky, I will glide silently, never making a sound
as I fade away into the night

More Photos

Grandma Marion with Grandkids

(L. to r.) Gabriel, Joey, Nathan, Jonah, Ariel, Jakob

Toddlers Jakob and Ariel

Ariel and Jakob

Extended family

Susan and Elya by the sea

Young Susan and friend Lee

Barbara, Lee and Susan

Nathan and Joey in San Francisco

Family in Sausalito

Paula and Marion in Sante Fe, NM

Jakob, Ariel, and Grandma in London

Bob, Jonathan, and Susan in Nantucket

Susan on first day of kindergarten

Jonah and Gabe in Sante Fe, NM

Bob in Bandolier, NM

Bob and Marion at Mass. Museum of Contemporary Art

When

When I can no longer dance
I will walk

When I can no longer walk
I will ride

When I can no longer see
I will hear

When I can no longer hear
I will feel

I will feel your touch
I will feel your love

Acknowledgments

Life is inherently risky. One big risk you should avoid at all costs is doing nothing. — Denis Waitley

I have taken the risk of writing this memoir anthology for my family and friends with the hope that they will find something of themselves in it.

My appreciation goes first to my parents who put up with my sensitivities and fears and who loved me without condition. They started me on a journey of love for books, art, theater, and dance.

Next, I thank my husband Bob who also puts up with my sensitivities and fears. We have shared an incredible journey, rich with family, friendships, art, music, and travel.

I thank my extraordinary children Jonathan and Susan, my true friends, who keep me young and laughing. They have in turn married the best people, Rachel and Elya, and given us six amazing grandchildren.

More than six years ago, I joined The Lawrence Writers Group. Our leaders Rodney and Tony have been dedicated instructors and nurturers, helping us all improve our skills. I can not forget my friends and partners in the group who encourage me with their praise and critique.

Finally, a note of appreciation goes to my best friends forever who put up with me, period!

You know who you are!